ADVANCE PRAISE

"I am a LEAPER! I thoroughly enjoyed Micheline Nader's book. She introduces the concept of LEAP, standing for 'Lean into your passion,' 'Execute from your purpose,' 'Align your mindset,' and 'Program your emotions.' As someone who has taught leadership in more than thirty countries for over twenty years, I found this book refreshing and authentic. The premise of the book is that as a leader, you need to start with deep self-reflection and self-motivation to understand your own personal passion, which you will then turn into your personal purpose and your personal mission statement. At a time when there is a plethora of books on leadership competencies, I found this approach inspiring. Her focus on humanity of leaders is a valuable contribution. I also found the book authentic. Micheline starts the book sharing her own passions and her own experiences. Every page of the book shows her sincerity and authenticity in trying to be helpful to others. Her helpful ideas don't just come from her intellectual prowess and her experiences. They also come from her heart. As I was reading the book, I couldn't help feeling her sitting in front of me, sharing her ideas. Another valuable feature of the book is how action oriented it is. She hand-holds the reader in making sure they cannot only understand the concepts but put them into action through step-by-step exercises."

—MANSOUR JAVIDAN, PHD, GARVIN DISTINGUISHED PROFESSOR AND DIRECTOR OF NAJAFI GLOBAL MINDSET INSTITUTE AT THUNDERBIRD SCHOOL OF GLOBAL MANAGEMENT AT ARIZONA STATE UNIVERSITY

"*This work is awesome! A step-by-step guide to developing leadership skills by interweaving business acumen, innate passion, and a clear sense of purpose.*"

—NICHOLAS GALAKATOS, PHD, GLOBAL HEAD
OF BLACKSTONE LIFE SCIENCES

"*What if consciousness could evolve at the same rate as science and technology? Dr. Micheline Nader assures us it can and must for the good of humanity. Her transformative work guides us to 'LEAP' to create a lasting legacy and a better future for all.*"

—JOANNA SHIELDS (BARONESS JOANNA
SHIELDS OBE), CEO OF BENEVOLENTAI

"*In Leap beyond Success, Micheline Nader draws on her own rich experiences leading and coaching leaders to take the engaged reader on an extraordinary journey of self-awareness and personal transformation. Nader's reflections on leadership are always insightful and stimulate thought, but Leap beyond Success goes beyond to provide a clear four-step approach for those looking to grow from personal success to creating a better future for all. Purpose is at the heart of this approach that applies to professionals across a variety of professions and industries.*"

—DEEPAK HEGDE, PHD, PROFESSOR OF MANAGEMENT,
NEW YORK UNIVERSITY STERN SCHOOL OF BUSINESS

"*For individuals looking at leading a purpose-driven career and life, this book is for you. Written by a sincere, accomplished, and humane leader in Micheline Nader, it will help you achieve meaningful personal and career success as you leap forward into your future life and sustainable legacy.*"

—FADLO R. KHURI, MD, PRESIDENT,
AMERICAN UNIVERSITY OF BEIRUT

LEAP BEYOND SUCCESS

MICHELINE NADER

LEAP
BEYOND
SUCCESS

HOW LEADERS EVOLVE

LIONCREST
PUBLISHING

LEAP BEYOND SUCCESS
How Leaders Evolve

FIRST EDITION

ISBN   978-1-5445-3689-7 *Hardcover*
      978-1-5445-3690-3 *Paperback*
      978-1-5445-3691-0 *Ebook*

I'm dedicating this book to you, the leader who wants to leap beyond ordinary success in business and in life. I hope this book will provide you with the tools to create from your passion a brighter future for all.

To my family and friends whose unwavering support makes me generate the unexpected.

CONTENTS

INTRODUCTION

The sound of sirens cut through the cacophony of shattering glass and splintering wood, the sharp crack of snipers' bullets, and the thunder of heavy bomb shelling. This was the soundtrack of a sleepless night of terror that I spent huddling in a bathtub, as far from windows as I could get. Our apartment building was being torn apart as Syrian and Palestinian forces targeted civilians and a nearby hospital in the Christian sector of Beirut. I already thought I had died multiple times that night. When the noise finally stopped, I dozed off for a split second but was awakened by the shrill ring of the telephone. It was a miracle that I was still alive—a miracle that our phone line was still working, despite losing the top floor of our building and all our windows.

"Good morning, Micheline, this is the American University of Beirut Medical Center," said the calm voice on the other end of the line. It sounded as if it was coming from another universe to the war zone I was living in. "The director would like to schedule an interview for a position at the hospital."

I stood in stunned silence. Was I dreaming?

The voice broke in again.

"Would you be able to interview tomorrow?"

I reminded myself to breathe. As surreal as it seemed, this was business as usual, continuing in the other part of the city, just fifteen minutes from our home.

"Of course, of course," I answered. "May I know which position I am interviewing for?"

At that moment, I'd have taken any job that offered a chance to get the hell out of my bathtub. But this was the most respected healthcare provider in the region, and the caller informed me that the job they were considering me for was Assistant Director.

I couldn't speak. Surely this was a mistake? I had just graduated from my master's in public health program a week earlier. But no—this prestigious institution really was recruiting me for a leadership role. Accepting that role would throw me into one of the most challenging positions I'd ever tried to perform.

But it would also help me discover, at a very young age, the leader I was born to become.

How does one discover one's innate capacity for leadership? The road is not always a steady progression of promotions over the course of a career or lifetime. Sometimes leadership is thrust upon us unexpectedly, and we rise to meet it.

I'd decided at the age of sixteen that I wanted to become a medical doctor. That was the year my dad passed away from cancer at the age of forty-two, and I took it upon my young shoulders to find a cure. I enrolled in medical school, but our dwindling family finances soon forced me to change my major to a Bachelor of Science in nursing. I had known my path lay in healthcare, but found my residency frustrating. Every time the patient needed something, I had to wait for a doctor's order.

Immediately after graduation, I enrolled in the public health school to major in hospital administration. My intention had been to go on to Johns Hopkins University after graduation, to complete my masters in Hospital Administration—until I got that fateful phone call that would fundamentally shape my professional life and perspective.

The University of Beirut Medical Center is the first medical institution in the Middle East with five international accreditations, including The Joint Commission, a not-for-profit organization that sets standards, evaluates, and accredits healthcare organizations and programs in the United States.

At the time, the center already handled more than 350,000 patient visits annually. For me, it was a baptism by fire. At just twenty-three years old, I became responsible for the operations of the hospital during the Lebanese civil war. Managing these daily operational challenges defined my leadership. Every day I discovered a new ability to learn and sharpen my leadership skills and prepare for different roles. No matter how much planning was organized into our regular meetings, emergencies trumped planning, and priorities were redefined by the crisis.

Managing emergency care, operating rooms, and medical supplies was a daily preoccupation. I learned not to sweat the little details, or to care about political affiliations, gender, or race. I kept my focus singularly on the patient's care. This was my *raison d'être*, which stayed with me throughout my career. That early leadership experience taught me to know what's truly important and what is not, especially in emergencies—and, as I experienced every day, during war. It also gave me the confidence and know-how to move forward in my career. I learned that no matter how challenging times are, I needed to keep focusing on the why (exactly as Simon Sinek advised in *Start with Why*).

Three years after I started at the American University Hospital of Beirut, I took on a senior executive leadership role at the American Hospital of Paris. Later, I became an entrepreneur, building several successful healthcare ventures in Canada and the United States. Then, I founded and led the Blue Dolphin Healthcare group, acquiring and managing skilled nursing homes facilities throughout the Midwest. At Blue Dolphin, I was on a mission to transform senior care through innovative quality care led by high-performance teams. To accomplish this, I recruited and retained a tremendous leadership team, and the company enjoyed a solid reputation among its stakeholders.

At the same time, however, I still dreaded many parts of my position, most notably the regular State inspections, the staff turnovers, and the constant risk of financial loss. Today, I can attribute this general anxiety and constant worry to my admittedly limited beliefs about setbacks. Only when I was finally able to break through my own limitations, my beliefs, and my reactivity was I finally able to let my business start to flourish and expand.

While improving my own executive skills was an important

key to my success, the biggest difference occurred when I empowered leaders and staff through the practice of conscious leadership. From top to bottom, our staff embodied a culture based on values of respect, integrity, dignity, and excellence. We created a framework of success that rewarded living these values, and focused on the principles described in the L.E.A.P steps.

Interestingly, a few months into these programs, we started noticing that the most successful innovators on the team were the employees who were engaged in their own personal growth. It turns out that the personal development of our staff had a direct effect on the quality of care provided, the bottom line, the degree of work satisfaction, and the well-being of our residents.

No matter where we are on the spectrum of success and fulfillment, we have an area of our life that we would like to improve. It could be in business, relationships, family, social life, service, or spirituality.

Over the years, I have encountered great leaders who mastered the art of achievement but lacked personal fulfillment. Some have reached retirement age, having accumulated significant wealth. Yet they are not satisfied with their life, despite the many things they can afford. Many amazingly smart individuals had big dreams yet were not able to attain them. Others made people around them successful, but never dared to leap out on their own to pursue their own dreams.

What about you? Do you believe you have attained your full potential? Do you, instead, have a knee-high list of regrets about your career or your business, thinking it is too late for you to embark on—or are you unsure whether your achievements matter? Alternatively, do you feel that you reached the success that you were aiming at, yet it still feels as if something's missing in your life, a dream still waiting to happen?

If you do, you are not alone.

If we were empowered to ask these questions frequently and early on in our career—especially before creating entrepreneurial projects and companies—we would be granted the opportunity of leading with awareness and impact every single day of our life.

Many leaders ask these questions a bit late in their life, when they realize that their success was not impactful enough. Do you know, for instance, that the inventor of the Nobel Prize, Alfred Nobel, was also the inventor of dynamite? Based on his work and patents, numerous explosive-producing factories were founded. Some of these explosives helped the construction industry. Some of them killed people.

Eight years before his death, he read his own obituary when a French newspaper mistakenly published it, instead of his brother Ludwig's. The obituary title was "The Merchant of Death is Dead." He then realized that his invention had a negative impact, and decided to leave all his fortune to benefit humanity. If Alfred Nobel had not read his obituary, would he have had this awakening? Alfred Nobel is not remembered as a merchant of death. Instead, he is celebrated as an agent of peace.

As for me, while I wasn't entirely reinventing myself like Alfred Nobel, I came to a point in my career when I found myself at a similar crossroad: either grow my business or divest it. I asked myself whether I would like to be remembered for the kingdom I've built, or for the passion that consumed my life and created my unique contribution and impact.

Because it was becoming more and more apparent that I was positively impacting my teams through my passion for self-development, growth, and personal transformation, I realized that I could affect leadership at a large scale by rendering this system for leaders outside of my Blue Dolphin Healthcare group. I divested my company, and dedicated my life to leveraging my passion for effecting personal transformation and leadership breakthroughs through my writings, workshops, coaching, and speaking engagements.

I've always been interested in conscious awareness and personal transformation. I attribute this to the many personal losses I suffered early in my life: I lost my dad (he died from cancer when I was sixteen years old) and my dad's business (a result of bankruptcy a couple of years before his sickness, when he lost a big shipment of construction material and the insurance company refused to cover it). I had to flee my country (due to the civil war that ravaged it a few years after my dad passed away). All these losses forced me to find a way to recover from them. I searched the fields of psychology and spirituality. I studied and participated in workshops. Through intensive seeking, learning, practice, and experimentation, I became aware that deep-seated beliefs and hidden fears entangle our potential, and prevent us from unleashing the extraordinary power within us.

Finally able to explore this in full, I set out to develop a system that allows tapping into our unfulfilled potential. A pragmatist at heart, I love nothing more than marrying introspection and prescription to create hands-on tools as a framework for individuals to live successfully, and to enjoy a life of personal fulfillment. Drawing on the conscious awareness and personal transformation lessons I leaned on throughout my life, I developed a simple and transformative system that can be understood and implemented by anyone motivated enough to affect change at a deeper level, at any stage of their career.

I called this method the DANCE process, which I outlined in full in my book, *The Dolphin's Dance: Discover Your True Self Through a Powerful 5-Step Journey into Conscious Awareness*. A comprehensive method for bringing conscious awareness to buried emotions, beliefs, thoughts, and behaviors, DANCE offers readers practical tools for accessing their unconscious beliefs, emotions, and patterns of behaviors to find the ones that hold them back, despite their conscious efforts. Through five simple steps, the book has helped thousands of readers and workshop participants generate "a-ha!" moments of realization and transformation, manifesting conscious awareness in every aspect of their lives. Six years since its publication, the book continues to resonate and help people today.

As I watched the COVID-19 pandemic turn people's lives upside down, I felt more passionate than ever about sharing these tools for leaders to find inner peace, outer purpose, and positive impact.

The pandemic forced the old paradigm to crumble and pushed the emergence of a new one. Leaders and individuals alike have started redefining themselves and their vision for the future. The question remains: are we capable of imagining a future from the future or are we creating a future from the past?

I believe that this moment is calling on us to leap beyond success and emerge from a future that is sustainable for our inner and outer worlds.

This book delves into that question and into the development of pragmatic tools to overcome the past and leap into a future of new possibilities.

All of this has motivated me to write the L.E.A.P. process, which applies the principles of conscious awareness to the field of leadership.

A self-improvement and leadership development guide, the L.E.A.P. process is written for leaders who want to leap into the next level in business and in life, whether they are looking to start their career or to cap it off with one final endeavor. It is written for leaders who want to master the art of self-development and social impact in addition to the art of achievement. Going beyond success requires going beyond execution—overcoming your past, creating a new future and, ultimately, going beyond yourself.

A four-step approach to uncover one's innate passion, unleash the leader you were born to become, and emerge into the future, the L.E.A.P. process is written for all kinds of leaders—entrepreneurs, solopreneurs, executives, and individuals—who do not want to stop at developing their leadership skills. They want to go beyond—to a different kind of leadership! They want to evolve. They want to move from being leaders to becoming Leapers. To leap is to create a passionate and purpose-driven life, a leadership envisioned from a future possibility, unencumbered by the past.

The four steps are easy to remember. Just remember L.E.A.P.:

- **Lean into your passion.** You will learn how to tap into your inner brilliance, define and put into action your personal vision, mission, and goals, and set yourself up for success.
- **Execute from your purpose.** You will find the tools you need to create a strategy and a structure for success, put together and nurture a high-performance team, and redefine your metrics of success to include a positive social impact.
- **Align your mindset.** In this practical journey into self-awareness, you will identify and transform the programs and narratives that prevent you from success and personal fulfillment. From there, you can create a culture that will bring forth the talent of your team members and help them grow, individually and collectively.
- **Program your emotions.** This game-changing step will unlock previously unrecognized emotions, and help you use them to create a conscious manifestation of your intentions.

Combined, these four steps will help you uncover and develop your innate leadership ability, and remove any obstacles to expressing your leadership in the world.

Most importantly, they prepare you to become an extraordinary leader as you leap beyond success.

01 Lean into your passion

Execute from your purpose 02

03 Align your mindset

Program your emotions 04

LEAP

As I was researching and developing these pathways, I found that the steps build on each other, following a natural sequence. However, the process is not linear. Development in any one area is linked to the expansion of consciousness in others. Once you master each step, you will find greater balance and aliveness in your leadership. Each step allows you to take guided action in the face of challenges, difficulties, and struggles. It also impacts your personal life, inviting you to feel more enthusiastic, more alive, more driven, more inspired, and more consciously aware.

I believe that we don't leave our personality at home when we go to work: we are the same person with the same identity, the same set of beliefs, and the same core values. We try to create lives and careers that reflect these deeper values and beliefs. And yet we don't always connect the dots. No matter how hard we try, our deep-seated beliefs and hidden fears continue to entangle our potential, and prevent us from unleashing the power we have to live extraordinary lives.

The secret to being a more effective leader, I discovered, is not *to do* more at once, but *to be* more conscious—a more self-aware person connected to your authentic self. I refer to this as conscious awareness-based leadership, and define it as an intentional process of transformation. It is a state of mindful and emotional wakefulness. It includes a deep understanding of one's own mindset and emotion-set, most notably beliefs, perceptions, and emotional prompts. It also includes a deep understanding of how some of these are unconscious and buried in the self, responsible for our reactive behavior. Fortunately, we can transform them to create the life and leadership we want.

The four-step L.E.A.P process will transform your leadership through conscious awareness and unleash the leader you were born to become.

CHAPTER 1

LEAN INTO YOUR PASSION

"There is a powerful driving force inside every human being that, once unleashed, can make any vision, dream, or desire a reality. My life's quest has been to awaken this force and help each of us to remember and use the unlimited power that resides within us all."

—TONY ROBBINS

Are you passionate about what you're doing? Do you wake up each day excited about the tasks ahead of you and go to sleep each night feeling like you've contributed to the world in a way only you can? The first step in this leadership journey is discovering your passion—uncovering the innate gift and talent you were born with, then learning how to leverage them to your advantage as you contribute to a purpose greater than yourself. Fostering your passion and then leveraging it creates a compelling mission for your life.

I've shared this essential first step of the L.E.A.P. process with people at every stage of their careers and life-journeys—from young adults in college to first-time entrepreneurs to senior executives. With young people, I've witnessed the profound impact it has on their ability to discover their passion and use it to shape their future endeavors, or simply to change their college majors. With more senior executives, I have been flabbergasted to see how impactful and transformational these ideas can be. Even the most senior leaders—the ones we all look up to—don't always give themselves permission to follow their passions and fulfill their dreams.

Many found this first step of the L.E.A.P. system to be instrumental in charting a different path to success. I certainly hope that it will similarly help you connect to the leader within to find your passion and purpose in life—the first step to creating an impactful, fulfilling career and leap beyond success.

Every journey has a beginning, and this assessment can help you determine your starting point. It can help you measure your progress as you move along the chapters and practice the suggested exercises. The assessments at the beginning of each step help you become aware of your areas of strengths and weaknesses as you focus on the first, and turn around the second.

STEP 1 QUICK ASSESSMENT: ASSESS YOUR ALIGNMENT WITH PASSION & PURPOSE

Rate yourself from 1–10 on each question. 1 = mostly false, 10 = mostly true.

1. I have a particular talent that is distinguished and unique to me.
2. I have created my career and my business around my passion.
3. I know what my purpose is in my life, and I integrate it in my professional endeavor.
4. I have created a purpose-driven career or business to contribute to and impact others.
5. I have a clear vision and intention for my life and for my future.
6. I have a personal mission statement that I live by.
7. I am known to be an expert in my field.
8. I devote time to practice my passion on a daily basis.
9. I have a coach or a mentor who helps me on a regular basis.
10. I consistently align my actions with my vision.

The maximum score on this section is 100 points. If you are between 90 and 100, congrats for being ahead—but you can still glean from this chapter and lean into your passion in most of your undertakings. You will be able to set an example for people around you, and coach them to connect and align with their inner genius. If you are below 30 points, that's okay; please don't be hard on yourself. Like many others, you may feel trapped in a career or stuck with a business you did not consciously choose. Perhaps it was someone else's idea; maybe you felt you had to carry on the family business. Maybe you've attained your goal, but are no longer sure you love your career.

Many of us hover between 60 and 90, depending on whether our actions and goals are at the service of that inner spark that makes us happy. It also depends on whether we think our passion is kind of an over-the-top dream that's unattainable, or is completely doable. I recommend that you rate yourself before and after you read this step to measure your progress.

The premise of my work is that when you lean into your passion, you become happy. When you start listening to what the universe is calling you for, you start tapping into the energy and momentum from your future.

I believe we each have some unique qualities which make us different. Our individual uniqueness—our essence—is something we were born with that differentiates us from everyone else. We each have an innate passion—a special talent, an "inner genius," that comes easy to us. Should you succeed in uncovering this passion, developing it, and leaning into it uninhibitedly in the world, then you will become the leader you long to be.

Your innate passion is the thing you love to do and have a special talent for. It is an inherent brilliance you have, a unique gift to you. Discovering your special inner genius is the key that unlocks your capacity for leadership.

We all have many passions in life—things we enjoy, things that fascinate us, things we're drawn to do, things we want to learn about. Sometimes, our passions develop as we grow, mature, and learn new things. Our innate passion is different from the many we develop in life, though it could manifest itself in these passions and activities we happily engage in and love doing.

Every human has a gift they are born with, a powerful innate passion associated with their uniqueness. It is a special talent, an inner genius. We each have the responsibility of untethering our innate passion and releasing it into the world. Our society and humanity depend on it. Once you uncover your innate passion, it will direct your actions and compel you to become the leader you were born to become. Once you align your actions with your innate passion, they will become more impactful in the world and, at the same time, lead to greater personal fulfillment.

Whenever we are inspired about something we are doing, creating, or contributing to the world, our consciousness expands, and latent forces within us come alive. Focusing these forces into a higher vision gives meaning to our actions. The key is to make use of the innate passion that we are born with.

Should you find a way to express your inner genius through your leadership, you will dance in harmony with yourself; you will be at peace and fulfilled with what is. This does not mean that you will stop growing. What it means is that you will be exceedingly successful while having fun doing it.

Your uniqueness is the positive power that propels you forward. If you harness this energy and express it with clarity, authenticity, and focused action, it will infuse your life and your work. Warren Buffett, one of the wealthiest investors on the planet, said, "At 85, I tap dance to work every day…because I get to do what I love with people I love, and it doesn't get any better than that."[1] His key success factor is his passion for what he does.

While I do not claim that you will join his rank simply by leveraging your innate passion, I do believe that uncovering,

---

[1]   Lydia Belanger, "Warren Buffet's 3 Top Pieces of Advice for Entrepreneurs," *Entrepreneur*, August 30, 2016, www.entrepreneur.com/article/277648.

developing, and leveraging it empowers you to find your purpose, and in doing so, become the leader you long to be.

Sometimes, though, our innate passion is hidden from us—buried beneath our fears, insecurities, or maybe our preconceived ideas about who we should be and what we should be doing. Other times, we may be aware that we have a special talent or passion, but we don't acknowledge or even think of it as something important enough to do anything with. Instead, we keep it as a hobby and attend to it, if we have time, or rediscover it after a midlife crisis or upon retirement. If we segregate our passions this way, we deprive ourselves of an amazing opportunity.

My childhood neighbor and friend, Michael, was a great guitar player. He was able to reproduce music that he heard without taking formal lessons. He did it effortlessly, not knowing how—it just came naturally to him. This was his passion. After we both moved out of the neighborhood, I lost track of Michael for many years. Recently, we reconnected. He had become a successful entrepreneur. In my memory, I always saw him with his guitar, so I asked him if he was still playing. To my surprise, Michael answered that he kept his childhood guitar as memorabilia, but had never played it since. I couldn't believe it. Yet, I understood. This is all too common for people to put aside a passion, forget about it, and pour their energy into mastering the art of business achievement and success in areas different from their natural talent.

After our talk, though, Michael picked up his guitar again, allowing himself some fun, playing every night even for just a few minutes. At first, it was just a form of relaxation but as most things you dedicate yourself to, it grew. The next thing I knew, he created a foundation to teach underprivileged kids to play the guitar! He's become a leader, inspired by his innate passion and leveraging his talent.

This innate passion is our inner genius—why would we not give ourselves the possibility of discovering, developing, and monetizing it early in our lives? The good news is—as Michael's story reveals—it is never too late to connect with and rekindle it.

To find your innate passion, start by looking at the activities that you enthusiastically involve yourself in and get absorbed by. Perhaps you will discover that your innate passion is threaded through these undertakings, projects, and hobbies.

Your innate passion is the energy behind your creative power. When you focus your energies on your innate passion, you move faster in the direction that you are heading. Your actions become meaningful; they propel you forward towards success.

Have you ever experienced being in "the Zone"?

When you are immersed in something you love, in your creativity, in the deep connection with something bigger than you, you feel as if you exist in a different realm of reality. What if you could create the Zone every day—as if you are connecting to the breath of life and anchoring it in your daily actions?

Recently, a friend and collaborator told me about how he started to move his passion into purpose. He always knew he loved telling stories—his own and other people's. While working as an editor, he enrolled in a Master of Fine Arts (MFA) program to develop his craft, writing his own stories and workshopping other people's stories to help them find their voice. Though it required a lot of time, discipline, and creative energy—not to mention money!—he never felt overwhelmed or discouraged, because he was feeding his passion and drawing energy from it. Though he still feels as if he's a work-in-progress, he has started to professionalize his passion by becoming a near-expert in developmental editing, and moving closer and closer to realizing his purpose through the same process I describe below.

Just as it did for my friend and collaborator, your innate passion can lead you to your purpose and allow you to be the leader you were born to become. For some, it may seem easier said than done. The truth is that it is not as complicated as it sounds. To discover your innate passion and bring it to life, you can use your intuition to guide you.

Whether you're someone who has been successful at your business but has never felt truly connected to your passion, or you are starting your career and are unsure what your passion is, you may find the following exercise useful and insightful.

EXERCISE: DISCOVER YOUR INNATE PASSION.

Step 1.

Sit quietly and move into a state of relaxation by taking a few deep breaths.

Step 2.

Write down the answers to the following questions:

- What is the thing you have loved doing since you were young and still enjoy?
- What could you spend hours doing without noticing the passing of time?

- What is the thing that you are great at, that comes to you easily, even effortlessly?
- What is the thing that you are particularly talented at and do better than most people you know?
- What is the desire or goal that, if you did not fulfill it in your lifetime, you would most regret?
- What is the thing that makes you feel alive?
- What are you yearning to do that makes you happy?
- What would you create in your life right now if your money, time, and resources were unlimited?
- What is the thing that you feel you can contribute to the world?
- What is your "dream come true" one day, some day?
- How do you want to be remembered?
- When you look back from your deathbed on your life and how you spent it, would you have regrets?

Step 3.

Read through your answers and notice whether you had the same answer more than once. If not, see if there is a general theme to your answers. The general theme points you towards your innate passion. The many things you are passionate about may have a common thread to point you in the direction of your special talent, your inner genius.

Step 4.

Write down your passions, and if you are able, describe your innate passion.

My passions are:

I have many passions in my life ranging from reading, writing, yoga, meditation, dancing, hiking, etc. My innate passion is to understand, demystify, and translate big ideas into pragmatic systems to better my life and help others do the same.

You might be passionate about something and even be naturally talented at doing it, but that doesn't mean you automatically have the skills and expertise required to turn that passion into a business or service that provides value to others. Once you identify your innate passion, you'll have to take the next steps on your creative journey, develop your skill set, and acquire the expertise necessary for success—from enrolling in a graduate program like my friend did, or finding a mentor like I did.

The most successful and accomplished leaders have a mentor and/or a coach. According to Bill Gates, everyone needs one. Those who can recognize, ask for, and find it will power ahead in pursuit of their personal and professional development. Famously, Steven Spielberg said that "the delicate balance of mentoring someone is not creating them in your own image, but giving them the opportunity to create themselves." Your coach or mentor will be able to guide you through your development needs, and bolster your abilities to reach your goals and pursue your mission.

At times, your mentor may believe in you more than you believe in yourself. I can remember many mentors who believed in me, including my college professor who hired me for my first job out of college as an assistant director at the hospital, and my banker who financed my first two long-term care facilities. In these instances, I had no idea what I was doing, or how I was going to do it. But my professor and my banker both believed in me. The beauty of our time and age is that expert mentorship is readily available—if we are willing to look for it—and it doesn't have to be someone in your immediate circle.

Remember, a mentor, leader, or boss can give you the *opportunity* to reach your highest potential, but never forget that the work is yours to do. By releasing the leader within, you can release the best version of yourself into the world and let it soar.

UNVEIL YOUR PURPOSE, ONE PASSION AT A TIME

Once you have found your special innate passion, you need to learn how to give it away. That is how you discover your purpose.

Your purpose is the intention behind your existence, your *raison d'être*, which gives meaning to your actions in the world. It is your connection to something bigger than yourself; it is also inherent to you. Your inherent purpose is the source of your innate passion. They both come together to bring your gifts out into the world. Fulfillment is the place where that innate passion meets your burning desire to contribute your purpose to the world.

Purpose is a loaded word, and some will shy away from it because of its spiritual connotations. However, you do not need to subscribe to any specific belief system to connect to something greater than yourself. It is not fun to be successful alone; it takes on a whole different meaning if successful leaders can help people around them become more successful. Purpose makes ordinary leaders heroes. It is the source of what some people refer to as charisma. They are driven by something bigger than themselves, which gives them the power to inspire others and the resilience to weather the storms.

Being committed to something bigger than yourself is a source of power and inspiration in leadership. In a certain sense, all leaders are capable of heroic actions, if they are driven by bigger visions. These are anchored in compassion, contribution, and service. When leaders are connected to the emerging future, then their goals and actions become meaningful. As leaders, they can generate daily actions that are aligned with the big picture, which become the source of our vitality and fulfillment.

If you look back at your life, you will see how your purpose has been unfolding all along. If you try to connect the dots of your many undertakings, you may see that your purpose was running through your life like a meandering stream weaving through the fiber of your most important accomplishments, following your own becoming. Following your purpose in life is like following the highest creative possibility of your own life.

From a young age, I was interested in these basic questions: Who am I? Where did I come from? And why am I here? When I look back at the common thread among all my life's significant undertakings, I realize that demystifying the big questions of our existence and integrating them into my daily living inspired and gave shape to my purpose: to constantly grow and develop my awareness, and to help people around me do the same, alleviating unnecessary suffering to live a consciously fulfilling life.

Aligning your passion with your higher purpose connects you to the greatest impulse behind life. It gives a deep meaning to your existence and a reason for pursuing your dreams beyond yourself. And it makes you a more open, more compassionate, and more effective leader.

Purpose connects us to a virtuous circle of energy and contribution. Our purpose becomes a contribution to evolve our organization and society in an impactful way. The more we contribute, the more we receive in return. The more we receive, the more successful and fulfilled we become. Purpose ceases to simply be a nice concept, and rather invites us to transform our actions at work. We enact a higher vision and challenge ourselves to become a better version of ourselves. Our leadership is no longer solely about meeting goals, but it is about embarking on a journey of self and team realization. Our teams are empowered, our organizations are impactful in a healthy way, and we become the leader we are longing to be.

For effective leaders to leap beyond ordinary leadership and become extraordinary, they must find their true purpose in life and express it authentically in actions, results, and impact. Purposeful leaders create purposeful organizations and contribute their innate passion to others.

Your innate passion can be expressed in multiple ways. You may express it through different projects or businesses, but your purpose remains the same. For instance, my purpose in life is to contribute to the wellness and well-being of mankind. I started by contributing through my role as a hospital administrator, a university professor, a long-term care operator, a serial entrepreneur in healthcare, a writer in self-development and leadership, and a motivational speaker. Coming from a place of contribution has given my life meaning, and made all my projects and businesses an expression of my purpose.

You may be asking, *What if I don't find my purpose?* Many people struggle to see it clearly, as I did for many years. The key is to abandon yourself to your many passions, one at a time, and play it full out with all you've got.

At one point, my passion was running hospitals efficiently and with great compassion and focused care. I played that passion out fully, from Beirut to Paris to Africa. Then I discovered another passion: long-term care. I wanted to take care of elderly people, especially after my grandma passed away. I developed the know-how, acquired the skills, and helped build long-term care facilities in Canada and in the Midwest.

Concurrently, I also developed a passion for personal growth. For twenty years, I participated in workshops, devoured books, and followed mentors. My own personal growth and development informed my leadership and improved it by leaps and bounds.

You may ask, *How are the many passions I develop in my life related to my innate passion and my innate purpose?* When you look forward to your future, your purpose is the path upon which your many passions unfold. Even if you can't identify your purpose or the meaning in your life right away, following your passions may afford you the fulfillment you long for, and over time, may reveal your purpose.

Take my friend Michael, for instance. Though he explored and cultivated many other passions in his life, he ultimately found his innate purpose by returning to his innate passion: playing the guitar.

When I was a teenager, I used to love visiting with our family friend, an unconventional Catholic bishop named Father Gregory. He had started a magazine to discuss his views about existence, consciousness, and spirituality. We used to spend hours in multi-generational discussion groups trying to understand the essence of who we are. This topic has been a passion of mine, which accompanied me throughout my life and my career. When I realized that I could become the cause in the matter and not only the effect of it, I became more accountable for my own actions and in identifying my own responsibilities for my choices, instead of pointing fingers at others or at circumstances. I became proactive in causing the change I desire, not waiting for something to happen in order to cause it. When I similarly understood that negative thoughts create my reality and not the reverse, I decided to create a system for changing my thoughts.

As I gained more knowledge about the interrelatedness of all things, I realized that the best way to affect change is to embody that change, become it, and render it accessible to whoever wants it. Thus, I developed a system to share with my teams. I became a stand-in for the team members' growth and development. I became aware that success does not occur in silos. For leaders, success is not fun if they don't bring their team and communities with them. The bottom line increased, so did our quality of care, our occupancy rate, and our retention of great associates. We all became more prosperous together, our salary and bonuses increased, and we were able to improve our programs.

Pursuing these different passions, no matter how loosely connected, helped me realize what my innate purpose is. When I look back, I can see that this passion to improve my life and the lives of others through practical applications of big ideas was always driving me. The key to uncovering it was to lean into my different passions one at a time, which empowered me to live from my purpose.

In the following exercise, you will learn how to convert your passion into purpose.

EXERCISE: UNVEIL YOUR PURPOSE.

Step 1.

Sit quietly and move into a state of relaxation by taking a few deep breaths.

Step 2.

Write down your innate passion that you uncovered in the previous exercise.

Step 3.

Write down how you want your innate passion to contribute to other people's growth and success.

Step 4.

Look back at your career and try to find a common thread, which may lead you to unveil your purpose.

Example:

My passion is to demystify big principles into pragmatic systems. Once I realized that I had this innate talent, I started living my passion through the different fields that I was interested in—from healthcare to wellness to self-development. My purpose in life is to contribute to these fields of interest. The common thread was to have different roles in health, wellness, and leadership, and contribute to the field of self-development through my writing, teaching, and speaking. My different passions, projects, and businesses were all an expression of my innate purpose, because my intention was always to add value to humanity, even when I was unconsciously doing it.

I hope the exercise above has helped you gain the clarity and the certainty of your purpose to experience a life that truly inspires you. If this exercise did not reveal your purpose, don't be discouraged. I tried to find my purpose throughout my career, and it wasn't until I started leaning into my passion and not worrying about it—creating my personal mission statement in action—that my purpose became clear to me.

ACTIVATE YOUR PERSONAL MISSION STATEMENT

Your personal mission statement defines who you are as a person, and connects your innate passion to your purpose by describing in clear and simple terms who you want to become. It explains your goal in life—your long-term vision as you dream things for yourself.

Once you have discovered your innate passion and unveiled your purpose, it becomes easy to construct a personal mission statement. This captures your vision for yourself and your goal for your life. It also spells out your innate passion and articulates your purpose.

Mission statements can change throughout your life as you lean into new hobbies and become interested in new ventures. While you will continue to acquire new skills throughout your personal and professional development, your purpose never changes; it simply finds different avenues of expression.

My purpose of making a meaningful contribution to people's well-being did not change throughout my life. Granted, it took different forms—first in hospitals, then long-term care, and, most recently, personal development. But as I started to recognize what all these ventures shared, I discovered my innate passion, which drove me to sharpen my professional skills and consciously develop my self-awareness to finally leverage my passion into an actionable goal. As a result, my mission statement has evolved over time.

My current personal mission statement:

To make a transformative impact in personal and professional growth to empower leaders to leap beyond success.

My personal mission statement connects my purpose of improving my life and others to my innate passion for understanding and simplifying big principles. It spells out in practical terms how I deliver this contribution to the world.

In this section, we will formulate a mission statement, so you are effortlessly pulled toward your vision for the future. Whether you are a stay-at-home mom, a visual artist, or a corporate CEO, your personal mission statement is important. It keeps you focused on your priorities in life. The activities, involvements, and projects you take on become a result of it.

Writing your personal mission statement is like setting your internal navigating system. It keeps you on track and prevents you from wandering off course. It will make your decision-making process easy. When you have an important choice to make, you simply ask the question: does this fit into my personal mission statement? If it does, go for it. If it doesn't, don't. If you are interviewing for a job or checking out a venture capital firm that might fund your startup, you can take a look at their business mission statement and determine whether it aligns with yours. If it doesn't align with your stated mission, you will know that this is not for you.

Activate Your Personal Mission Statement

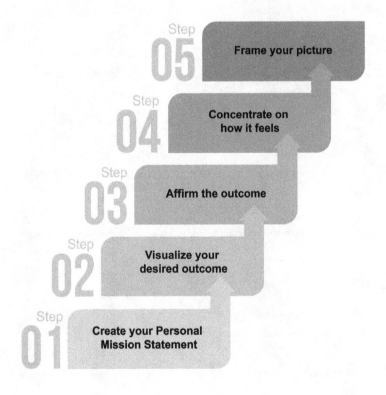

Step 05 — Frame your picture

Step 04 — Concentrate on how it feels

Step 03 — Affirm the outcome

Step 02 — Visualize your desired outcome

Step 01 — Create your Personal Mission Statement

STEP 1. CREATE YOUR PERSONAL MISSION STATEMENT.

Your personal mission statement—which, for memory's sake and maximum impact, should be ten words or fewer—is like your personal mantra. It's a good idea to post it where you can see it daily and share it with people around you to keep it alive.

EXERCISE: CREATE THE PERSONAL MISSION STATEMENT

Step 1.

Write down the answers to the following questions:

- Who do you want to be? Example: *a leader*
- What do you want to be known for? Example: *inspiring followers*
- What will be the benefit that you want to create for others? Example: *to lead from their passion*

Step 2.

Put your three answers together to formulate your personal mission statement:

Example: To be a leader who inspires followers to lead from their passion.

Step 3.

Write your mission statement in the present tense as if it has already happened—to intensify your intention:

Example: I am a leader who inspires followers to lead from their passion.

STEP 2. VISUALIZE YOUR DESIRED OUTCOME

Think about eating a hot pepper or a lime. If you can imagine yourself eating the hot pepper or the sour lime and experience the pungent or sour taste in your mouth, then you relive a past experience and imagine a future experience through visualization. Ask your mind to bring up a good memory from your past and see if you can relive it.

When you visualize, you create a picture in your mind. The closer the picture is, the clearer you can imagine it. The more you can sense it and feel it as real, the more your subconscious believes it and your mind creates it.

Visualization has been and continues to be practiced in sports. Many athletes use the power of visualization as a way of programming their minds to win. Baseball players may repeatedly imagine the perfect throw; tennis players, the most accurate serve; runners, a personal best that gets them across the finish line ahead of all others. And it's not just in sports. Many successful people believe in the power of visualization. They rehearse their talk before it happens. They run their meetings in their mind prior to attending.

I usually visualize my presentation before I begin my workshops. Whenever I take the time to do that, I get better participation from the audience and more positive feedback on my delivery.

By focusing on your personal mission statement and taking a few minutes in the morning and in the evening to visualize it *as if it already happened*, and since your subconscious mind doesn't differentiate between whether something is real or imagined, the exercise generates the belief that it already happened. This will propel you to make it happen, and your deeply held desire will come true.

You can create the desired image in your mind and feel how life will be when you have fulfilled your wish. You can picture yourself in the future and the people around you: how achieving your goal makes you feel, how people are reacting to you, and what positive impact your offering will have on them. Visualize the impact you desire. You can imagine the scene as if it were a movie of your life playing itself with a final image representing your success. You can frame that image, surround it with white light, and bring it to your memory as you are rehearsing your success daily.

I use this technique during or after my meditation first thing in the morning, and before I close my eyes at night. You will be surprised at the results of this technique, and how powerful it is to create and manifest your dreams.

Visualization entails picturing an image of yourself as you are achieving your goal or living your passion.

You can choose any goal that you would like to achieve—big or small, one that is derived from your mission statement or a small one like exercising or lifting weights. Whatever you choose, it should be a goal that you deeply desire or are passionate about.

You can visualize what the outcome will be after your goal is achieved and your wish is fulfilled.

STEP 3. AFFIRM THE OUTCOME.

Visualization requires a calm state of mind and a willingness to activate your imagination. You can begin by taking a few deep, calming breaths and imagining your own body and mind relaxing as you visualize a tranquil place of your choice. It could be a beach, mountain, meadow, or calm lagoon. I like to imagine my body relaxing as I breathe in white light and breathe out stress and negative thoughts.

Imagine it in your mind, and affirm that it has already happened. Create a visual image in your mind's eye by imagining how your life is going to look when this happens—after your dream is fulfilled.

STEP 4. CONCENTRATE ON HOW IT FEELS.

Embody it, feel it, and get specific. Center your attention on all the different aspects of fulfilling your dream—where are you? What is the place like? Who are the people around you? How does it make you feel to be there? What colors do you see? What sounds do you hear? How does the air feel on your skin? What's the view like? And, finally, when it's complete, how does it feel to know you've accomplished your aspiration? Seeing it play out in front of your eyes like a movie or a video is highly effective in the subconscious mind-programming process.

STEP 5. FRAME YOUR PICTURE.

You're looking at your picture in the future after you've achieved what you wanted—the way you want it to be. This step is a static image—a view of your life *after* your desire is manifested. Describe this image in detail: Who are you with? Does this picture have colors? Where are you? Can you frame it in your mind? Can you increase the intensity of the colors? Can you change the colors as you please? Can you imagine it up close? Framing your picture, the way you want it, is also highly effective to program your subconscious mind.

EXERCISE: FROM VISUALIZATION TO MANIFESTATION

This is a practice exercise to visualize and manifest your desires, vision, mission, passion, and purpose. It will lead you to success, abundance, wellness, fulfillment, and impact.

Step 1.

Sit quietly and move into a state of relaxation by taking a few deep breaths.

Step 2.

Think of a success story or a big achievement you accomplished in your past. Remember the powerful emotion. Relive it by visualizing it and describing it in as much detail as possible. Feel into that moment, that experience.

Step 3.

Extract the powerful emotion, hold on to it, and attach it to your new goal.

Step 4.

Feel the feeling when your new vision is achieved. Exaggerate the feeling.

Step 5.

Every time you think of your goal, bring up the feeling of success and link it to your goal.

Step 6.

Decide to buy something that reminds you of your achieved goal and frame it in a place that is visible to you when you start your day, and you are working.

Step 7.

Visualize and affirm your goal achieved, first thing in the morning and last thing before you close your eyes.

Congratulations! So far, you have worked to uncover your innate passion, discover your purpose, and construct a mission statement that can guide you forward. You have started leveraging your passion to benefit and help guide your life and undertakings. However, until you experience your passion and purpose in action, they will remain conceptual. To continue leveraging your passion, you need to turn it into a benefit for you and others, which requires you to execute your purpose.

In the next section, you will learn how to turn your innate passion, your purpose, and your personal mission into a project or a business. Executing from a place of being will create a life of limitless success and impact.

KEY TAKEAWAYS

Fulfillment is the place where your innate passion meets your burning desire to contribute your purpose to the world. To lean into your passion is to:

- Discover your innate passion.
- Unveil your purpose.
- Construct your personal mission statement by capturing your vision, passion, and purpose.
- Practice visualization to activate your mission statement.

CHAPTER 2

EXECUTE FROM YOUR PURPOSE

"I want to be thoroughly used up when I die, for the harder I work the more I live. I rejoice in life for its own sake. Life is no 'brief candle' to me. It is a sort of splendid torch which I have got hold of for the moment, and I want to make it burn as brightly as possible before handing it on to future generations."

—GEORGE BERNARD SHAW, *Man and Superman*

Despite your work thus far, your innate passion, your purpose, and your mission statement are not enough to create the success and fulfillment you long for in your life. How can you align your actions to your purpose and turn them into success? The answer is simple: *execute.*

Many people can talk about inspiring ideas and visions, but execution is what differentiates mediocre leaders from great leaders. Those who fail to execute their passion-driven purpose do so because they either did not clarify their intention, did not commit to the hard work it required, or did not engage other people in the journey. What allows you to succeed is your intention and commitment to leveraging your passion and aligning your work through your inspired actions.

This step is a very significant one. Whatever project or idea you want to create, execution is the key, and great execution is a learned skill. To create the impact you want, you can't take the journey towards it for granted and neglect the means of getting you to where you want to go.

Before we delve into the tools to execute and put your purpose into practice, I would like to share an example of a purpose-driven execution.

On November 26, 2019, my husband, Francois, called me from Boston's Logan Airport while waiting for his flight back home. He was excited to be offered the opportunity to serve on the board of Moderna. He joined soon thereafter, having no idea that the worst pandemic in modern times was already brewing, or that he would be asked to serve on Moderna's COVID-19 board committee, which oversaw the development, manufacturing, and distribution of the vaccine—in short, how much of a life-changing assignment it would be for him!

The virus, which had already deprived so many people of their breath of life, was developing at stunning velocity. It laid bare the fallacy that life is predictable. Every day brought unprecedented challenges: closing offices, manufacturing plants, colleges, and schools; downsizing; furloughing; firing staff. There was no obvious blueprint from which to draw. Trial and error became the plan of many.

We were globally observing and experiencing things that seemed surreal. Despite the numerous warnings from our scientists about the likelihood of such a pandemic, we were globally ill-prepared and sadly witnessing the failure of society's effectiveness. Leaders of every industry started navigating the crisis with uncertain actions and decisions, yet a small Boston-based biotech company rose to meet the challenge.

The COVID-19 pandemic was already raging through China and the world unrestrained, when on January 11, 2020, China shared the virus's genome sequence and scientists jump-started developing a COVID-19 vaccine. Because Moderna had been preparing for a moment like this for ten years, it was ready to take on the challenge. Just two days later, Moderna had sequenced its mRNA vaccine, and by March 16, the first subject received its COVID-19 vaccine named mRNA-1273, as part of a phase 1 trial, which included forty-five subjects. This was flawless execution in action: after preparing for ten years for a D-Day-level event, it took Moderna only sixty-four days to convert a viral genome sequence into a vaccine that would end up saving tens of millions of lives.

How did this happen? How was a small biotech company able to add immeasurable value to the world's health and economic assets, to its stakeholders, and to the global economy?

At the 2018 FAST Conference in Oakland, California, Noubar Afeyan, cofounder of Moderna, gave a speech, in which he said one has to embrace the process of "Foresee—Foretell—Forereach." What he meant was that we need to envision something valuable and seemingly unreasonable from the future, and communicate it in a way that current stakeholders can understand and get behind. We then need to take steps to make it happen. In other words, we need to reach into the future and bring it alive in the present. He warned that it may get uncomfortable and challenging, and we may fail. But he also noted that to leap, one must be able to fail.

For Noubar Afeyan, Moderna's success wasn't so much a bolt of inspiration out of the blue, but rather an *unreasonable* starting premise from the future. Programming a messenger RNA, and prompting the body to respond to it and protect itself, was certainly not a reasonable starting point for experts and analysts. "Most breakthrough innovations are descendants of unreasonable starting premises," Afeyan said. "We should not work on things that start life at a proven, understandable, relatable starting point, where some expert tells you it's a good idea."

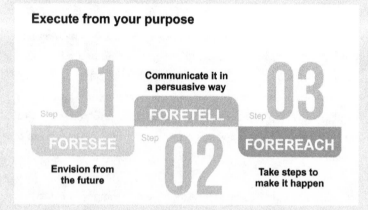

I believe Moderna exemplifies its purpose-driven implementation every step of the way—leading from a future vision and creating the execution from that vision.

While the pandemic represented an opportunity for Moderna, the recognition that people were dying every day, in every single corner of the globe, strengthened everyone's sense of purpose in the organization. Working endless hours to get it right became more than just a job or an ambitious project. Working to achieve this goal became a personal mission to save the world. This was Moderna's Big Hairy Audacious Goal—no matter what it took. When you envision a goal from the future beyond yourself that you Foresee collectively, and you Forereach to make it happen through purpose-driven execution, you and your organization will leap beyond success.

WHAT IS YOUR BIG HAIRY AUDACIOUS GOAL?

For some, it might involve creating a product or offering a service. For others, it is turning their life's purpose into a message, and monetizing it by empowering people into transformational breakthroughs. Here are just a few examples:

- After she battled breast cancer, my friend Sylvia ran a successful fundraising campaign for cancer support. Because Sylvia's purpose is about serving others, she found a new mission through service to help cancer patients.
- Judy, a successful hairstylist, launched a self-funded project offering free service to clients suffering from hair loss. She turned her life-long struggle with alopecia into her personal mission, aligning it with her passion for styling hair.
- When Oprah Winfrey founded OWN, her network, she did not need it to become more famous. She wanted to teach and inspire people to be more than they think they can be. Her career took off in the late 90s when she started a series of "Change your life" shows. She herself overcame a difficult and abusive childhood to become an unprecedented motivational anchor who inspired millions of people to do the same. Today, she is one of the ten richest self-made women in America.
- Louise Hay started the Hay House publishing house in her sixties. After she was diagnosed with cancer, Louise put her beliefs into practice by publishing her first book, *Heal Your Body*. Her passion for serving others translated into everything she did. As a result, Hay House became a

leading publishing house in its genre, bringing in big-name authors like Wayne Dyer, Suze Orman, Joe Dispenza, and Jerry and Esther Hicks, to name just a few.

You can create and monetize a business out of any innovative idea—or as Afeyan put it, any breakthrough descended from unreasonable starting premises. Sylvia wanted to raise money for people suffering from cancer. Judy wanted to give men and women battling hair loss the same dignity and self-expression her other clients enjoy. Oprah wanted to help people change their lives. Louise Hay wanted to change conversations and invite new voices into them. None of these were exactly reasonable starting premises, but each woman realized their breakthrough in innovations through a series of measurable metrics.

Like any other successful person, when you put your dedication, commitment, discipline, skills, and action behind your idea, and when you surround yourself with the right people, you can succeed. People who have achieved boundless success, impact, and fulfillment are those who connected with their innate passion, aligned it with their purpose, and executed from it.

The key to this limitless success is marrying your passion and your purpose, which empowers your actions and motivates you through any challenges you might face as you work to achieve your goals. When you get to create within the sandbox of your passion, work becomes play, and your purpose and passion find a way to be expressed through your endeavors.

Already, we've learned how to leverage our passion and start to unearth our sense of purpose. We also emphasized the importance of executing from our purpose, which can only occur when our personal mission and actions line up.

Since finding a solution for the global pandemic was a compelling cause for each and every one at Moderna to rally around—from the CEO to the chief marketing officer and everybody in between—every single employee found a great personal meaning in racing to develop a vaccine that would literally help millions of people around the world. All at once, Moderna found meaning and a purpose in what they were doing. Everyone was aligned, which resulted in an example of a purpose-driven execution.

Wherever I present or lead workshops, oftentimes participants share how much they are longing to do something professionally and/or creatively that satisfies their personal mission. This is especially true of the younger generation of leaders and of individuals who would like to create a legacy. Should an organization's purpose and mission be meaningful for you personally and for your staff, the execution of a well-aligned business plan becomes smoother and more impactful. What seemed an unreasonable idea from the future finds its way to reality if the proper structure of satisfaction is put in place.

In the sections that follow, I will share some tools to help you master the art of a successful purpose-driven execution, whether you are an entrepreneur just starting out, or a leader looking to pivot and align your work with your newly revealed purpose. There is no such thing as a flawless execution, but rather an enjoyable journey towards achieving goals and exceeding them. In doing so, I will describe some implementation techniques which include metrics of success that every generation of leaders continue to recognize and value as sound leadership practices—like SMART and SMARTER techniques (more on this later). Such evergreen metrics complement a new generation of techniques, allowing you to make sure your personal mission is always aligned with both your professional passion and your business's larger purpose. You can then Forereach what you Foresee for yourself and for your business.

All roads may lead to Rome, but only a select few will help you guarantee the kind of purpose-driven execution the stories in this chapter demonstrate. So, let's see where you're beginning this leg of your journey.

STEP 2 QUICK ASSESSMENT: HOW WELL DO YOU EXECUTE ON YOUR PURPOSE?

Rate each question on a scale from 1 to 10. (1 = mostly false, 10 = mostly true)

1. When I set a goal, I achieve it 100 percent of the time.
2. I created my career around my passion.
3. I am known for being a visionary leader.
4. I set an intention, commit to my end goal, and achieve it.
5. I clearly identify my career objectives.
6. I always meet my deadlines and I am always on time.
7. My personal strategic plan is aligned with my career strategic plan.
8. I have goals for my immediate future, the next six to twelve months, the next five years.
9. I use a system to track my goals, measure my success and priorities.
10. I celebrate progress and success every step of the way

Your maximum score is 100 and your minimum is zero. No one scores a zero or a hundred. Where are you on a scale of 1 to 100? Less than 30 percent, around 50 percent, more than 75 percent?

If you are below 30 percent, chances are that you procrastinate or get frustrated trying to meet deadlines.

Like all the assessment questionnaires in this book, I do recommend that to measure your progress, you rate yourself before and after you read this step to measure your progress.

START WITH YOUR INTENTION, THEN COMMIT

Many wise teachers have taught some variation of Paulo Coelho's quote from *The Alchemist*: "When you want something, all of the universe conspires in helping you to achieve it"—to which I would add: "so, don't forget to let the universe know what you want!" Too often, we jump into action without taking the time to set a clear intention. So, while this section of the book is focused on action, we must begin with setting and committing to an intention. You can do this for a new business, for a specific project, or for improving something you're already working on.

The more aligned your intention is with your personal mission statement, the more likely and more powerfully you'll succeed. Your intention will not only help you create your business or boost your career, but it will also help you fulfill your dreams and goals. What would you like to create that will enable you to continue doing what you love? You may have many passions through which you might express your purpose. Setting an intention forces you to choose and focus.

Think of your purpose in terms of a state of being, and think of your intention as a personal vision for yourself that you want to attain to fulfill your purpose. Getting a new job, a promotion, or creating a business or venture capital firm occur as a by-product of your state of being in your purpose and living your passion. Your actions originate from your purpose and your innate passion, not vice versa.

It is essential to set an intention. It makes you state what you want and communicate it clearly. It is like setting a direction in your GPS. When you set an intention, you create an attractor that can pull you toward it. As the saying goes, "Where attention goes, energy flows, and results show." Setting a clear intention redirects your attention. If you set an intention and you believe in it, your actions will align with that which brings you closer to your intention.

Your intention precedes setting a goal. While setting specific, measurable goals is important (we will come to that later in this section), your goals must be preceded by a clear picture of where you want to end up.

If you let your purpose inspire your actions, and if you let your intention guide you to your outcome, success takes a different meaning. Goals are easier to commit to if they are seated in a bigger vision.

When you think about your intention, ask yourself what you would like to achieve for yourself and your life through this process. Your intention should always be about yourself, never about someone else. It is also important to choose your intention from within, and make sure that it was not chosen for you by someone else. It should be yours and yours alone, even though you may choose to have partners who may share or align with it, and are eager to help you execute it.

It is important to ask yourself why this intention is meaningful to you. How will you feel about achieving this intention? How is this connected to your purpose and mission statement? Is it your dream vision or someone else's? Too often, people pursue a dream that was impressed on them by their parents or people they look up to.

Dig deep to ensure that your intention is not coming from someone else's idea. In his book *Millionaire Success Habits*, Dean Graziosi describes a method that involves asking repeatedly, "Why is that important to you?" until you reach the root of your motivation.

Your intention should be clear, inspiring to you, coming from within, and something you believe in. It is hard to inspire, motivate, and enroll others if your vision and intention are not clear. It is also hard for you to commit to your intention if your vision is not clear and you don't believe in it.

Your intention should be positive. Although intentions point us towards the future, using the present tense instead of the future tense helps us set our intentions in motion right now. As I mentioned earlier, your brain does not distinguish what is current and what is future, as long as you are convinced and believe what you are telling it. Set an intention as if it has already happened in the now. Here are a few examples:

- If your passion is gaming and your purpose is about educating others: *I am a leader of educational virtual games.*
- If your purpose is to contribute to people's lives and your passion is to play music: *I am a leader of inspirational music.*
- If your intention is to attain a higher level of leadership and your passion is to mentor leaders: *I am a leader in mentoring conscious leaders.*

Setting an intention for your leadership will allow you to measure your progress and success in a tangible, meaningful way. While you know and believe your intention to the fullest, it's important that you let go of any attachment to a specific form the outcome should take. In doing this, you open yourself up to possibilities you may not have imagined yet. Your intentions will change throughout your career. Opportunities will arise, but if your goal is to create passion in your life, you have to start by expressing your passion. Contributing your passion to the world attaches meaning to your actions, and creates a purpose in your life.

Visualization is a powerful practice of manifesting your passion and purpose. Visualizing that your intention has already come to fruition is like rehearsing a possibility from the future—believing that it has already manifested in your life.

For example, if your intention is to create a resort and spa business, see it in your mind, with all the details you can imagine. Picture yourself living there with all the beautiful sensations you can create. Rehearse the feelings that are arising as your intention is manifesting. What does it *feel* like? Keep rehearsing that image through each phase of your project—as you plan and take action towards executing your vision. The more positive the belief and sensation in the present moment, the more powerful the manifestation.

Allowing yourself to imagine what your life will be like when your intention materializes—in one, five, or ten years—will help you bring that feeling forward as a realistic possibility. Who will be the people associated with your business? What will the effect be on them and on you? What will the effect of your success be on the people closest to you? What will the effect be on the people you care about? What will be different in your life if your intention is fulfilled? Who will benefit from your talent? What will be the impact of your actions on your family, community, organization, and the world you live in? On your own sense of self?

Once you have set an intention, you must commit. You must accept the call to action. Rise to the opportunity you have created and implement your intention. Accepting the call to action, of course, is also accepting the possibility that you will fail and have to start again. It is committing to work through all the setbacks and struggles you will encounter.

Are you in? Are you ready to commit? Are you wanting it badly enough to accept going through the tests, the setbacks, the trials and tribulations in your daily practice? Are you ready to let go of the old way for a higher level of leadership to occur? Do you have enough passion to "chop wood, carry water," as the Zen teachers say? In other words, do you have enough to do what it takes—even the most mundane things—to realize your intention and achieve your goals? Are you willing to keep going, knowing the moment you start acting challenges will arise? People and systems will test you; they will resist your efforts to change. And your own patterns and modus operandi may agree with them. It is the greatest challenge to keep believing in yourself and in the process for this transformation to become a way of being. Are you ready to face the challenges that will come your way? If you answer the call to action, you need to have a statement of commitment.

Write your statement in the following form:

EXERCISE: START WITH YOUR INTENTION, THEN COMMIT.

Step 1.

Write down your intention. My intention is _____.

Example: *I am a leader of educational virtual teen games.*

Step 2.

Ask yourself the question: What would it be like for me if my intention materialized? Visualize yourself and your life when your intention is fulfilled. Feel the emotion that the fulfillment of this intention will bring to you. Connect with this feeling every time you think about it. It is like planting a seed—you will nurture it every time you think about it.

Step 3.

Display it on your desk or in a visible place.

Step 4.

Visualize your intention. Pause and visualize your intention already manifested in your life. Take a few deep breaths and quiet your mind.

Close your eyes and try to feel that innate passion of yours. Feel the feeling of doing it in the world. Feel the emotion of success that comes when you are singing your deepest song. Visualize yourself doing it on a large scale. Rehearse it. Exaggerate the feeling of happiness. Visualize the white light showering you while doing what you love to do.

Step 5.

Commit. I commit to (one...) new action every day that moves me towards creating my intention.

SUCCESS BY DESIGN: A FRAMEWORK FOR FULFILLING STRATEGIES AND GOALS

Success rarely happens because of luck. If it does, it is probably not destined to last. Whether professionally or personally, for enduring success to happen, you need a strategy. You need to build a structure of achievement to satisfy the strategy of your goals, one step at a time.

In the Lean into Your Passion chapter, you uncovered your innate passion and purpose, which informed your personal mission statement. And, as part of learning how to Execute from Your Passion, you've figured out how to set an intention and commit to it. Together, these two steps are pivotal for success.

Success by design, then, requires you to build a structure that empowers you to set the strategy for achieving your desired outcome and directing initiatives that help you do so—even before you get started in earnest.

Once you set your intention and commit to it, the following steps will help you realize your vision faster and check off the "traditional" metric of success every leader, regardless of industry or generation, considers necessary for a thriving enterprise. While SMART and SMARTER goals (more on this later) are effective and universally accepted metrics, I will also introduce you to easy-to-implement markers of success that have an immediate impact.

Say you want to develop a product or open a restaurant. Either way, you start with a strategy, which spells out the chronology of your actions. You need a strategy even before you write the action plan for your business. Strategy differs from an action plan, because it spells out the reason and priorities for what you do.

Attracting the right talent to join your project, and finding the right fit, are key to bringing your vision to fruition. Earning their trust will allow you to inspire organizational members into agents of change, committed to helping you realize it. You may not be ready to start hiring people yet, but you can test out the idea by creating a mastermind group. Your mastermind group is your think tank, the team that helps you brainstorm the feasibility and creation of your idea. Enroll your mastermind group in your idea. Some of them may become members of your advisory board. They can help identify and recruit other team members, all of whom possess different skill sets and areas of expertise that will help you execute your passion—in this case, opening a restaurant.

Once this is accomplished, you start looking for the restaurant you would like to buy, the building you want to rent, or the land you want to build on. While the architectural plans are being created, your builder can start costing out materials, applying for permits, ordering the materials, and hiring the construction crew—all in parallel.

A robust strategy is fundamental for the success of any venture, whether your organization is for-profit or not. When Moderna committed to its goal of developing a vaccine against COVID-19, for instance, they crafted a strategy for every step. This ranged from the sequence of the vaccine itself, to the funding of the clinical studies; from the input of its mastermind group and other key stakeholders, to the recruitment of volunteers for their clinical studies and FDA approvals; from manufacturing the vaccine, to its worldwide distribution.

Your long-term strategy is usually a three- to five-year plan. From this plan, you derive your annual plan, and articulate your set of strategic goals and priorities. When you can see where you are going in three to five years, it's much easier to understand where you need to be in the next twelve months. Which of the key thrusts and capabilities need to come first? Which have the greatest priority?

The selection of the strategic priorities of your organization is a crucial step. You need to design a process suitable for your organization. It could be done by a committee of experts, market consultants, or simply your mastermind group or your board. This committee of experts will work with you in selecting the idea or ideas that would advance your field or business. Selection of these priorities is based on, among other things, competitive data and competing companies that offer similar products or services.

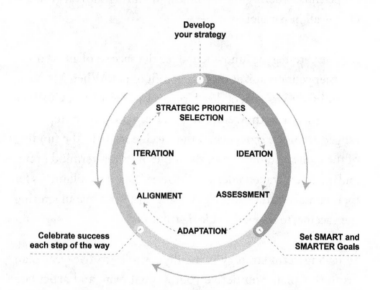

What makes an execution model succeed or fail lies in the process itself. Those companies who took their execution to the next level, and created a flawless one, have paid substantial attention to the following phases:

1. **Strategic Priorities Selection:** It could be a committee of experts, market consultants, or your board—this committee of experts will select the idea or ideas that can advance your field or business based on regular brainstorming sessions. The selection of these goals is based on competitive data and comparative companies that offer the same product, services, and businesses.

2. **Ideation:** Generate, select, and develop the sequence of ideas that move from the original concept to implementation. The chronology of the action plan should be discussed and evaluated. For this step, I recommend that your operational team be your best execution group.

3. **Assessment:** If your process yields a successful idea, it is important to capture the critical success factors for repeatability purposes. However, many ideas can fail. If they fail, your assessment of the causes of failure is imperative in order to determine if you should try the process again in a different way, or let go of it.

4. **Adaptation:** Adaptation is a crucial step for innovation and the creation of novel ideas, products, and services. (A successful idea may need periodic updates, requiring some form of adaptation of material, delivery, or timing.) Failure does not always mean the idea was bad. It could simply mean the process needs to be changed. Or that, in order to execute, you need to adapt the idea and the process to your core competencies, or develop new ones.

5. **Alignment:** Aligning the project to the organization's mission and purpose is key. If the project is also aligned with your personal mission, a nice momentum for success is generated.

6. **Iteration:** Repeat, improve, repeat. Through iteration, you can continue the momentum of progress and innovation. Through variations, companies create more success, answer the market needs, and stay relevant.

Looking at the Moderna example, you can't help but notice that the company aced the above-mentioned six phases. The strategy and ideation were impeccable. Assessment was constantly made through the clinical studies metrics from a percentage of protection against COVID-19. With each metric, an adaptation was made possible through testing the different dosages and cadence of booster injections, then administering the vaccine and distributing it. Part of the adaptation was to create different manufacturing sites in various countries, and to deal with the different government agencies as well.

The urgency of the global pandemic helped align all their staff, management, and executives to their mission. Everyone had a personal stake in that mission whether vaccines were their passion or not. It was for their own survival, their family's, and the world's. Their cheerleaders were the whole world. This is the most compelling example of alignment. This is how the crisis has ignited a leap into the future and created a new possibility, one which had not happened before: the first application of an mRNA technology effectively and safely on a vaccine creation.

GET SMARTER AND FIND YOUR WINS!

Many people fail because they neglect to *smartly* organize their energy and effort towards a goal. Goals provide the energy one needs to carry on, even when motivation is low. Having a goal gives you something to focus on and work towards. It propels you forward, and constantly reminds you of what you desire to achieve.

Well-thought-out goals and objectives help you achieve the best possible result. If you want your goal to become a reality, and not end up in the bucket of unfulfilled dreams, you really need to think and execute in a smart way. To start, your goals have to be aligned with your mission statement—both your personal one and, if relevant, your business one.

The most commonly used methodology for goal setting is the SMART technique. First developed in 1981 by George Doran, SMART stands for Specific, Measurable, Assignable, Realistic, and Time-related.[2] Over time, people have adapted the terms to represent their own vision. Some like to use Attainable instead of Assignable. I prefer the latter, because I can assign sponsors and track the progress with one person. Mapping the end-goal backward helps create certain milestones that you can use to measure progress. I also like to use Relevant instead of Realistic, because I find that in our day and age, we must constantly stay relevant.

Relevance is about the real benefit attached to reaching the goal. Evaluating why the goal matters—to us, to our clients, and to our organization—is critical. Relevance compels us to innovate and helps us compete in a noisy market. It appeals to our creativity and passion, which motivate us towards attaining our goals. Achieving our goals needs to be within a certain time frame. When the goal drags, it loses its impact and its relevance.

Some people have expanded the acronym to SMARTER, incorporating two additional criteria: Evaluated, which means you assess your progress; and Reviewed, which means that, if necessary, you adjust the approach to reach a goal. Adopting the SMARTER technique gets you closer to the framework of success by design that I described earlier in this chapter.

---

2   George T. Doran, "There's a S.M.A.R.T. Way to Write Management's Goals and Objectives," *Management Review* 70, no. 11 (November 1981): 35–36.

In my previous company, the Blue Dolphin Healthcare group, we implemented this structure of success by design. We established our annual goals according to our business priorities, from which we derived the operational tactics and identified key performance indicators (KPIs) for achieving measurable progress at each milestone. We listed the resources we needed to meet our goals and appointed a contact person, who we called the Sponsor, accountable for coordinating the efforts towards that goal. To ensure that everyone in the company was aligned, the same system was implemented at each of our Blue Dolphin's Long-term Care facilities. We generally had our annual meeting in early December. Our leadership team would meet for a full two days, during which every operational head and corporate officer would present their accomplishments of the year based on their goals. The second day was devoted to assessing the organization's strengths, weaknesses, opportunities, and threats along with our critical success factors. This would inform the design of the operational and financial goals of the upcoming year. The leadership teams of our different long-term facilities were invited to participate in the working sessions. Each operational unit and the corporate office presented their five annual goals. During these two days, quite a bit of time was also devoted to breakthrough sessions of sharing, transformation, and culture building. The whole team believed and were enrolled in the company's shared vision.

What is the secret sauce to achieving getting SMARTER, beyond goal setting and implementation?

Each one of us needed to find our wins. What are the "wins" for our patients, their families, the staff, our enterprise and our shareholders? All the stakeholders had to win. What would be the social impact of implementing our strategy? This had to be a win as well.

Once everyone identified their wins, they could align their personal vision of success with the organization's vision of success. Being a social impact- and performance-driven organization, the performance reviews were a critical component of aligning the individual performance with the company's.

So, how did we enroll the stakeholders in our vision?

Once we recognized everyone's win and incentive, it was easy to come up with an enrollment strategy. When people are enrolled in their own vision and aligned with the organizational vision, synergies happen, and exponential growth occurs. Challenges turn into opportunities; pursuit of excellence becomes a byproduct of the increased impactful engagement of all. Effective teams and meaningful relationships are built. Less time is spent bickering and gossiping, and more effective group communication occurs because the primary focus is not on oneself, but on one's mission.

Our team was engaged in how to improve the quality of care and the well-being of our residents. We started the first wellness program in Oklahoma's nursing homes, from alternative to complementary to inte- grative nursing care. We offered a multidisciplinary approach to living: nutritional wellness, psychological support, herbal medicine, art and music therapy, friendship circles, prayer groups, therapeutic massages, internet-based programs and connections with loved ones, etc.

We provided transformational training to our employees as well as an employee assistance program focusing on wellness and well-being. These training sessions were crucial to our progress. They also entailed enrolling our stakeholders, empowering our teams, communicating clearly, living our core values, listening, measuring success at each milestone, and getting the necessary feedback to adjust.

During our bi-weekly leadership team meetings, not only did we report progress, but we also discussed any challenges we faced on the personal and professional levels. I remember one of my directors telling me that she looked forward to our leadership team meetings because of the breakthroughs that we shared together. The team felt heard, empowered and motivated to pursue their goals, innovate, and create models of care. As a result, our nursing homes found their niche specialties. For instance, one excelled as a skilled rehabilitation nursing center with strong ties to the hospital. Another one became the Geri psych nursing center of choice in the state. Another one innovated in Alzheimer's care. When we decided to remodel some of our facilities, the facility team took on the project and collaborated together to make it happen. It was amazing how the teams coordinated the projects, and completed them in a timely manner. Those who work in the long-term care field know how difficult this could be, given the staffing challenges. But together as a team, we felt stronger every day to face them. As a result, our quality of care soared along with the satisfaction of our residents and our staff as well. We were having fun while working hard and growing personally and professionally. The team members were able to design their success and the framework we had in place helped them create it.

While this approach is widely used, the way you implement it, and how you use it, determines how you achieve a smooth execution. You can create your own strategy and structure for success. It does not matter what you use or what criteria you include. The most essential thing is to create a strategy that takes into account your needs. It should be consistent with your scheduled meetings, encouragement, alignment, and communication of the clear goals and the progress to create the momentum!

If you are clear and aligned with your vision and mission, the universe will always have your back. I was always positively surprised how, when I brought my dream forth into reality, invisible doors opened, creating the unthinkable and the limitless. From each goal, you will derive many tactics, as many as you need. What seemed to work for us was to keep it simple and limit our goals to five or six. It is a common pitfall to want to cram the timeline into the first part of the year. However, it is more realistic to spread it evenly, depending on the priorities and ideation of your developed strategy.

EXERCISE: PRACTICE SETTING ONE PROFESSIONAL GOAL BASED ON THE ABOVE FRAMEWORK.

Step 1.

Select the Strategic Goal based on the description above, making sure the goal is aligned with your mission statement. Why does this strategic goal represent a priority for your business? Write it down as a goal in your template. Example: *Expand geographic territory to increase product sales.*

Step 2.

Develop the sequence of actions from the original concept to implementation. Write them down as tactics in your template. This is part of your ideation process. Example: *Recruit two additional sales members from the specific target territories. Train them. Incentivize them. Etc.*

Step 3.

Develop metrics to measure the goal attainment at each milestone. Write down the appropriate metrics and cadence. Example: Increase sales by 5 percent from the specific territory in the first six months and 10 percent by the end of the year.

Step 4.

List the resources needed. Write down all needed resources for your goals. Be as specific as you can. Example: Budget, training, personnel.

Step 5.

Write down the name of the person responsible for coordinating and following up on the steps of the goal. These are your sponsors.

Step 6.

Develop a cadence system for a status report at each milestone. Write down the method of reporting. Example: *Scheduled meeting, reports.*

Step 7.

Assessment and feedback. Schedule meetings and a feedback system for Evaluation, Adaptation, and Iteration as described above.

CREATE MOMENTUM USING THE DOPAMINE EFFECT "EN ROUTE TO ACHIEVING GOALS."

While SMART and SMARTER goals are effective and universally accepted metrics for success over the long-term, I also like to consider more immediate and smaller wins as indicators of progress.

For starters, I like to create momentum, and I always remember to have fun.

Throughout history, people have looked to their leaders for

guidance, especially during trying times. This is exactly the kind of guidance needed to implement success by design. One of the leader's essential roles is to reassure their followers by tempering fear and negative emotions, and by driving emotions toward positive outcomes.

A study conducted by the Yale University School of Business showed that emotions are contagious. Good moods have direct implications on business outcomes. Moods influence how effectively people work; upbeat moods boost cooperation, fairness, and business performance. The study concluded that "emotions may spread like viruses," noting that laughter, smiles, and cheerfulness spread more easily than irritability and a bad mood. To paraphrase the study, laughing is often the shortest distance between two people, because the shared experience instantly interlocks their limbic systems.[3] The interpersonal limbic regulation is described by scientists as the "open loop," whereby we transmit and receive emotional signals from each other that can affect functions in our body such as hormonal, cardiovascular, and sleep rhythms.

According to Dr. Andrew Huberman, a neuroscientist at the Stanford University School of Medicine, achievements, courage, the pursuit of goals, motivation, procrastination, and burnout are all linked to dopamine. Dopamine and serotonin are important neurotransmitters, both of which regulate moods. There is a link between dopamine and how you experience pleasure. Dopamine is also associated with drug addiction, because it helps drive behavior towards things that can activate the pleasure center the same way it drives behavior towards achievements.

---

3   Sigal G. Barsade, "The Ripple Effect: Emotional Contagion and Its Influence on Group Behavior," *Administrative Science Quarterly* 47, no. 4 (December 2002): 644–675.

When we overcome a stressful event in an adaptive way, it triggers the release of dopamine, which makes us feel better. This could range from standing up to a condescending boss in a civil way, overcoming a fear of heights or a fear of failure, to a more heroic act. It is referred to as the courage circuit.

The same thing happens when we reach a goal: we release dopamine. Since this biochemical makes us feel good, it is considered as a reward for reaching the goal of overcoming a challenge in a successful way. It also reinforces successful behavior, creating new pathways in the brain, which make us engage in that behavior again. That same pathway's circuit could get triggered in the future.

Dr. Huberman finds that dopamine is also released "en route to achieving goals." It allows us to achieve actions despite the uncertainty of the outcome and the long periods of time that might take to attain them. This neurotransmitter helps you renew your motivation and replenish your drive on your way to your pursuit of dreams. Why is this relevant? Progress towards reaching a goal goes deeper than one would think. It affects our physiology. Celebrating the steps to reaching your goal will make achieving it even sweeter because dopamine is secreted all along the way! That dopamine release is needed to re-activate motivation. So, if you want to use the dopamine release system intelligently, you celebrate your little wins and encourage your staff, colleagues, and partners to do the same.

I used to jump from one achievement to the next goal immediately, without taking a breather. Now I stop, give myself a pat on the shoulder, indulge in (shhh) a delicious piece of chocolate, and go for a walk. I might even jump up and down for a few minutes or do the happy dance. (Why not? Just don't let your boss see you! Or maybe they'll join in with you!)

Happiness is contagious. Just celebrate, even if it is for a few minutes, and luxuriate in the positive effects of even the smallest of wins. These are your milestones and will help renew your drive and motivate your teams for higher performance. Registering these wins is essential. Use them to achieve your end goals, but also to register moments of thankfulness and appreciation towards your teams, colleagues, and partners. And remember, studies have shown that dopamine deprivation—not registering wins along the way to the end goal—could lead to burnout and depression.

You and your team will most likely re-engage these same pathways of success, thus success breeding success becomes an active process of your organization. The reverse is also true: you can also create pathways in the other direction, which will cause dopamine depletion instead.

Dopamine is also released as you move forward towards a challenge. Bungee jumping, skydiving, and ziplining have been used in leadership training. As people walk on a narrow line between trees, they learn how to confront and overcome certain fears. That often translates into gaining mastery over their fears of public speaking or finding the courage to confront their boss in a constructive way. As you are moving towards the challenge, that forward move itself at the peak of anxiety and arousal triggers the activation and release of dopamine. This neurochemical plays an important role in the reward mechanism, which reinforces the willingness to engage in the same behavior again. This explains how courage begets more acts of courage and bravery.

This also is the cause of why some people experience depression or a big letdown after they reach their goal or after an exam, a pitch, or a project that they've spent a long time preparing for. It happens to me sometimes after I deliver a big successful workshop or a talk. When it does, I immediately turn to my toolkit for replenishing my dopamine stores, which consists of spending time in activities and with people who make me happy—like being with my kids, my husband, and my furry companion.

If you are a high achiever and building a high-performing team, it is important to reward achievements and celebrate milestones every step of the way. This is important, as we create our framework of success matrix, to make sure to capture the milestones and the metrics. Tracking progress and celebrating wins is key for success.

Burnout happens when the reward does not come in a timely manner, does not come at all, or is disproportionate to the achievement. In sales, often the reward comes only if the salespeople achieve their goal. However, if they work hard and aren't acknowledged for their efforts, they can easily burn out, especially if the goal was out of reach and not realistic in the first place. The same applies to any team member when they work hard and are not rewarded. Blame it on the Dopamine!

PRACTICE EXERCISE

List some routines and rituals to celebrate milestones and successes, and plug them into your calendar. Think of the places you like to go to celebrate with your team and the activities that are fun and make you happy. Plan them even before each success happens.

In addition to celebrating major and minor successes to foster a happy environment in which everyone can thrive, it's important to generate and maintain momentum, which triggers a similar Dopamine-induced response.

Momentum is the most essential ingredient to creating limitless success, and the biggest hurdle we face en route to success.

So, how does one build on the momentum to achieve success?

Acknowledging progress every step of the way, and attaching a positive emotion to the milestone, build on the momentum. If we follow the psychology of achievement and the dopamine factor, we understand that celebrating progress is mandatory for creating a sustainable philosophy of success.

At Blue Dolphin, whenever we had annual or bi-annual meetings, we made sure to celebrate our wins, big or small, acknowledging our accomplishments and impact, before we began to assess our goals. At the year-end meeting, we always wrapped up with an award recognition dinner. We made it a point to invite leadership teams from each nursing home to a celebratory lunch, during which they were debriefed on our progress, vision, and destination.

These celebratory moments set us all up for the upcoming year, from the board members to the entry-level employees working as a unified group—confident, motivated, and in good spirits. Simple and fun, these celebratory moments foster an emotionally aware culture, which allows everyone to thrive and bring their authentic selves to the shared mission.

The key is to identify small, consistent actions towards the goal, and to not let unexpected obstacles sidetrack you. These small steps stack on each other. Like the fire in your fireplace, to keep it going, you keep stacking the wood. The velocity at which you add the wood pre-determines the strength of the fire.

On the other hand, if you stack a giant piece of wood on top, you may kill the fire. This is what happens with big goals. Some start with a big bold action and, if that fails, it can kill the momentum. Starting small, and building up from there, is the best way to keep it going.

It's important not only to create momentum, but to sustain it by taking consistent actions until a goal is reached and beyond. This can be done, for example, by regularly scheduling meetings to follow up, give progress reports, resolve any obstacles in the way, and solidify the next steps necessary to keep the motion moving forward.

Celebrating progress is a fun step on your journey of execution. It is an exciting and happy step towards fulfillment when we take time to pause and express gratitude to the members of the team for working hard. It supports achievement, is an antidote to failing to keep the morale up, and genuinely recognizes the effort of the people who are playing full-out. While success is a team effort, each member has a critical part to play in that success.

Having fun and celebrating the team increases their level of satisfaction. It sends a strong message of appreciation to your team. Momentum is the key to growing a business. When the business grows, it is important to recruit consultants and coaches to help support the growth and sustain its momentum.

You can't celebrate success or generate momentum, however, without empowering your employees.

EMPOWER, ENGAGE, AND CREATE A HIGH-PERFORMING TEAM

Creating a high-performing team starts by hiring the right people.

Empowering your existing employees as essential members of the team makes them feel secure in their respective positions, and confident in their abilities to contribute in a meaningful way to short- and long-term goals.

Conversely, not having a sense of safety or belonging could lead to feelings of anxiety and insecurity—and thus, the wiring of the fight-or-flight response. Our health and wellness can also be impacted, because our deep issues with safety and belonging affect our nervous system. The feeling of being unsafe puts us on edge, and we tend to react to the threats in a significant manner. An environment like this is more like a toxic environment, which cries out for more compassionate, smarter, and focused leadership, which will encourage more committed team members.

Feeling safe allows us to express our ideas, try new approaches, and innovate without fear of being penalized or ridiculed. It also allows us to be truthful and upfront when we make a mistake, own our failures, and not blame other people for them. If you feel that you are not acknowledged or appreciated at work, you need to ask yourself this question: *Am I feeling unsafe because of previous conditioning, or are the feelings warranted because of the organization I work for?*

To belong is to feel like we matter to our team, that we belong to a tribe, and we can readily celebrate one another's successes. When it comes to the fulfillment scale at work, the feeling of belonging matters much more than salary increases. Feeling that we can lead effectively and belong increases our desire to improve our team and the organization we work for.

If you feel that you're unable to become the leader you know you can be, if you feel that your team doesn't respect you or have your back, or if you feel they are uniting against you, it's time to take a good look within and ask yourself some important questions.

Do you feel that you contribute something of value to the organization, but your efforts go unnoticed? Do you feel you must constantly prove that your job is important, and that you're capable of leading the team? It may be time for you to step back and reflect on what's going on within you. Ask yourself, first, if perhaps *you* don't feel you're good enough. Then, see how that and other things might be contributing to the situation that's playing out in your life.

EXERCISE: DETERMINE YOUR ENGAGEMENT AND EMPOWERMENT.

The following exercise applies to you and to your staff equally. You can both benefit from determining your engagement factor. Ask yourself and your staff to answer these basic questions?

- Do I feel safe? Do I belong?
- Is my personal vision/goal/mission aligned with the organization?
- Do I have a development and growth plan?

Often our perception of being unsafe—especially if it's a pattern of ours—comes from our past and may not necessarily be how we truly feel now. To test the validity of your answers, ask yourself the additional questions that follow. The answers to the questions are personal; you do not need to share them with your team. Should you decide to share your answers in a context of safety and trust, your answers would probably help you and your team recognize the value of building a culture that would increase the sense of belonging in the organization.

Ask yourself:

- When did I feel unsafe before? Write your answer down.
- When did I feel unsafe before that? Write your answer down.

Keep going until you can't find other situations.

Look at all these situations and see if there is a link. If so, what is it? Write this down, too.

I had one of my staff leaders do this exercise. She discovered that she felt unsafe when her boss was a woman, and yet she felt very safe working with a male boss. She established that her relationship with her mom was the link. Since she was reporting to me, we came to an agreement that the only way she could work with me was for her to be able to process her feelings, and for me to be a stand for her to break through her feelings of insecurity. Her fears did not go away, as her wounds were deep, but we were able to enjoy years of a beautiful relationship, and got to a level of workability we would not have been able to access otherwise.

Getting to the root cause of our patterns of feeling unsafe helps us maintain a healthier nervous system. It takes a toll on us to be constantly in a fight-or-flight response. Being on edge for small or big events will have consequences to our health. Therefore, understanding our conditioning and reframing our past becomes more than a luxury. It becomes a necessary uncomfortable step that can give us access to being a different kind of leader—someone who understands the importance of a group's emotion-set, and can regularly engage and empower employees by making them feel safe and valued in their workspace. By celebrating success, we can generate momentum.

THE KEY ELEMENTS TO A HIGH-PERFORMING, THRIVING TEAM

While goals, tactics, and moves are the pillars of execution, what makes the execution flawless is developing a high-performing and thriving team, totally aligned with your vision. When action comes from a vision bigger than us—and when the team is aligned with the vision and is in service to others—it generates a momentum that is hard to stop. Here, then, are my six keys to developing a high-performing team, and how to practice them.

The key elements to a high performing thriving team

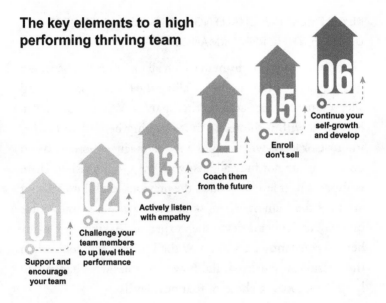

KEY ELEMENT #1: SUPPORT AND ENCOURAGE YOUR TEAM.

Support your team with resources and believe that they can do it. I always felt that the staff needed me to believe in them, sometimes before they could believe in themselves. When someone they admire holds a fierce stand for their potential, it is contagious, and their mind shifts towards success. We can all think of instances where we did not believe that we could handle a task, but someone else believed that we could. As a result, we progressed to the next level. To stand for who they are going to become on their journey is what really matters. Sometimes, I could see them become successful even when they doubted themselves, the same way my first employers saw that success in me and gave me the opportunity to realize it. This is empowerment in action.

KEY ELEMENT #2: CHALLENGE YOUR TEAM MEMBERS TO UP-LEVEL THEIR PERFORMANCE.

Hold a vision for your team in which all members can become a greater version of themselves. Calling the team to progress and success makes them step up their games. When momentum is created within the team, those lagging behind will either improve or leave, which is not a problem since those who end up leaving are not fully aligned with the group's vision. There is always a next level that takes the previous levels into account, arranges the team members' skills and experiences, and builds on them to further develop their expertise. Asking team members to constantly envision how the business will look when the mission is actualized, and how their roles will change, will keep them looking ahead to that next level.

KEY ELEMENT #3: ACTIVELY LISTEN WITH EMPATHY.

Imagine yourself in their situation—put yourself in your team members' shoes, and make them feel safe on their path to the next level. This is critical. Active listening helps you communicate at the level of the person listening to you. It facilitates building trust, resolving conflicts, and understanding the other's ideas and points of view. It improves productivity as communication becomes clearer, and you can both grasp the message as the communicator intended it. Team members, colleagues, stakeholders, and bosses will tend to be more authentic with you if they know that you are a sympathetic, engaged, active listener.

Active listening is a prerequisite for enrollment and sales as well. The same way you have to listen to what your team members want in order to help them attain it, you have to actively listen to your clients' needs in order to offer them your product or service.

Paraphrasing, reflecting meaning, and validating are all techniques of active listening but for me empathy trumps them all. Listen deeply to the possibility of who your team members want to become. Should you become a stand for them to achieve their role while aligning their actions with their mission and the business, you will unlock a powerful key to develop a high-achieving team.

KEY ELEMENT #4: COACH THEM FROM THE FUTURE.

When you are conscious of your team members' struggles, you can become the one who sees that next level and holds them to it. You can get comfortable with their discomfort and inspire them, becoming the transformational leader coaching them from the very future that they aspire to.

Shannon was recruited as an administrator to one of our long-term facilities. She did not have a lot of experience, but she certainly had potential. She underwent comprehensive training in her new position, and we partnered her with Linda, one of our experienced administrators. Demonstrating our trust in Shannon's capabilities, Linda worked directly with Shannon on site for the first two weeks, mentoring her on our values, mission, and core purpose, as well as on operations. Shannon continued to work under Linda for the first three months.

Once Linda earned Shannon's trust, she challenged her to step up her game. She coached Shannon to believe she could accept new challenges and, in the process, accomplish more in her position. From time to time, Shannon doubted her ability and struggled to embrace this challenge, a concern she shared with her mentor. After listening to Shannon, Linda constantly assured her that she was already doing a great job, and motivated her to reach the next level.

Over time, she started outperforming some of her colleagues and was promoted to leader. Within months of her promotion, in terms of quality she brought her nursing homes to triumph over the competitors. Her numbers and metrics followed, and her team exuded confidence and happiness, which mirrored the reaction from her patients. Shannon's skilled nursing home team became the flagship of our chain. She found her purpose in executing a high level of care, building a great team, and creating efficiency in her operations. As part of our leadership transformational workshops, she was able to successfully implement the two first steps illustrated in this book.

Building a deeper connectivity with the team as a leader pays big dividends. As leaders, most of us did not learn to become executive coaches, yet we all play this role with our subordinates. If you have the means, recruit consultants to help you improve these skills. I found that companies that use these talents are better prepared to create high-performing, thriving teams.

EXERCISE: PUT YOURSELF IN THEIR SHOES!

Step 1.

Make a list of the people on your team, in your department, or in your network whom you would like to connect with.

Step 2.

Every day for the next week, pick one person from your list and connect with them, either in person, via phone, or through a video platform.

Step 3.

Practice active listening. Just listen with compassion. Be with the person and connect with them by trying to understand where they are coming from. Try not to give your opinion, but just practice listening.

Step 4.

Imagine you are the person you are listening to. Imagine their biggest dream. Imagine their biggest fear, and feel with them.

Step 5.

Every day write in your notes what shifted for you with that person as you stepped into their shoes.

As a leader coach, you can help your team clarify their immediate goals and long-term vision for themselves, and recognize the challenges that keep them stuck.

Here are some things that you can help your team recognize:

- What their leadership goal has been until now
- What issues they have had to deal with in leadership
- What might have frustrated them and kept them stuck
- What they are trying to achieve in their life

- What this achievement means for them as a possibility they can ascertain
- What their life will be like if they achieve that

Great leaders help their teams see the progressive stages of achievement, and they recognize and reward team members every step of the way. They connect with their teams, they root for them, and they become their biggest cheerleaders on their way to success.

You build a high-performing team by showing team members support, challenging them to up their performance, and actively listening to their fears, doubts, and concerns—with empathy. You recognize and honor their inherent dignity by helping them execute their responsibilities—with excellence.

KEY ELEMENT #5: ENROLL, DON'T SELL.

You want to empower team members and help them see how everyone, regardless of background or experience, can evolve. You can achieve this by constantly enrolling them into a future possibility. Regardless of your position or title, you constantly have to enroll people into your idea, product, service, project or vision. In order to enroll them, you need to understand how their beliefs about the idea, product, service, project, or vision align with yours.

I used to think that enrollment was registering for school or signing up for membership, until I enrolled in a Landmark course and started practicing enrollment as means of communicating possibilities. For the purpose of this work, I like to define enrollment as follows: listening and communicating future possibilities to people. It is making people feel and visualize what their life will be like when they acquire what you are offering them.

If this experience is what they are looking for, they are enrolled in the benefits they want to experience, which also benefits you. If they discover that the experience is not what they are looking for, then they would not be a "good fit," and you both part ways. Whatever the outcome is, it is a win-win situation for them and for you.

The same applies to your customers as you are building a sales organization.

Most people fall in love with their own ideas or ventures—but this is not enough. To become highly successful, they need to *fall in love with the people they serve.* When you enroll, you are not selling an idea, project, product, or a service. You are connecting people to the benefits they'll receive when they bring your offerings into their life.

To be connected at that level means aligning what your team members want with what your business needs. You want to be able to put into words, for your team, what you believe to be true—to demonstrate that you understand, at a deeper level, what exactly they want.

People want to be led by someone who they feel authentically has their best interests at heart. And you want to be true and authentic. If you are manipulating people and selling them an idea that is against their principles, they may fall for it for a while, but sooner than later, they will figure out the game and will drop out as quickly as they got in.

You become a more conscious leader when you help your team members go from where they are to where they truly want to be. Not only will you fulfill your promises, but you will also exceed them. What makes a team a high-performing one is when the metrics show that the deliverables are aligned with the goals, and the customers are highly satisfied.

The same enrollment principle applies to your potential customers. If you are selling a service, help your potential clients see, feel, and visualize the benefits of this service. This is called your value proposition, and it goes beyond delivering more than you promised.

The more you understand the people you serve and can speak to their needs, desires, and dreams, the more you become the leader they turn to. When you master the art of providing benefits for others in your target market, you become their most trusted advisor.

We all know that the proof is in the pudding. Let them experience the service and, if it doesn't meet their expectations, offer them a way out. You can't master enrollment if you can't master respecting people's option to say no! Mastering enrollment entails giving your team and whomever you are enrolling the opportunity to reject what you are enrolling them in.

Mastering enrollment is also mastering the art of telling the truth, authentically. If you build your teams around authenticity, you will never sell people services they don't need or services you can't offer. With every sale, you have the possibility of impacting their life so that they can impact the lives of people around them. With every sale, you have the opportunity to play full out in your own purpose and help them to play full out in theirs.

Basically, you have to listen actively to your target audience and be genuinely interested in them. To enroll people in what's in it for them, you have to be genuinely interested in their lives, their hobbies, and their families. The more you care about them, the more they will connect with you. The more interesting they find you, the more they will be inclined to listen to you. The more you actively listen to them, the more you can help them articulate what they are trying to achieve by enrolling them in your project or your ideas and buying your services. What are they achieving? Why do they want it? What does it mean to them to achieve it? And how do they progress towards achieving it?

If you then feel that you can help them better than other alternatives, you will be in the best position to offer people what you believe is best for them and tell them why you believe it—giving them every element they need as genuinely and as sincerely as possible. Through this process, you become their greatest champion and advocate for the needs of your clients, your team members, and your colleagues.

When the needs of the market align with your value proposition, it creates a greater potential for winning. When this same alignment occurs between the team and the organization, you are successfully enrolling high-performing employees in the organization's mission, which makes teams unstoppable, and future expansion becomes exponential.

EXERCISE: PRACTICE ENROLLMENT IN LIEU OF SELLING.

Everything you want to sell is enroll-able, if you can present it from the point of view of the person you are trying to enroll and if you can take into consideration their biggest concern and biggest goal.

Step 1.

Grab a pen or a notepad and think of something important to you that you would like to enroll another person in. It could be something you want them to get, an idea, or a project. Usually, it is an idea, a vision, or a transaction. Write it down.

Step 2.

Think of a client, partner, colleague, team member or boss you are trying to enroll. Write down their name.

Step 3.

Write down why it is important for you to enroll them in it.

Step 4.

Put yourself in the mind of the other person, and write down why it is important for them to get enrolled in your idea, vision, or transaction.

Step 5.

Do you know their biggest fear or concern? Do you know their biggest goal? If not, would you be able to guess or find out?

Step 6.

Write a sentence you think will grab their attention, taking into consideration their fear and their goal. This is referred to as a hook. Try to empathize with their fear and cheerlead for their goal in the most genuine and authentic way. Think and feel as if you are them. Feel what they feel.

Step 7.

Tell your story and the benefits you got or you will get from that idea, project, product, or service. If it is a vision, imagine all the benefits you can reap from the idea and plan to ask them if they feel the same about it. When you are preparing and rehearsing this exercise, prepare for each possible answer.

Step 8.

If their answer is no, back off and don't enroll. Instead, acknowledge their position, and close the discussion by letting them know you understand this may not be for them, or the timing may be off. If their answer is yes, proceed to Step 9. Again, this is a rehearsal that you will implement in person afterwards.

Step 9.

Write your compelling offer: What is it you are offering? What is your value proposition to them and all stakeholders? How would they feel if this were to come to fruition? How would this impact their life? And why are you the best coach/leader to offer it to them? How do you compare to others who have the same vision or a similar product?

Step 10.

Write it down. Try to limit all this to five sentences: **The hook, your story with their benefit and outcome, why you are the best alternative, your best possible offer, and why the time is now.**

Example:

Hook: Do you want to spend your next ten years on the road or confined to an office from nine to five with a fixed income?

Story: I was that way once, bored in a job that I didn't choose. Today, I am passionate, motivated, make higher bonuses, and look forward to waking up every morning. The benefit for you will be to learn skills, develop expertise, and move your leadership up to the next level.

Compelling offer: Today I am offering you free training with an increased bonus and a guaranteed outcome in the next x months.

Now that you have rehearsed, go out and practice. If you don't get the result you want the first time, practice delivering with more empathy, compassion, and non-attachment to the outcome. I guarantee that you will surprise yourself.

Enrolled yet?

KEY ELEMENT #6. CONTINUE YOUR SELF-GROWTH AND DEVELOPMENT.

I've enjoyed leadership roles throughout my career, built reliable teams that grew with the business, and had a few surprises along the way. For instance, some great managers lost their stamina and unassuming ones rose to the opportunity and became stars. I'm sure you know people who seem to have their plans all figured out, got to be very successful, and then lost the important things they had in their life for things that were not so important. They may have jeopardized important relationships for their careers. They may have achieved great success and then found themselves stuck again in undesirable patterns of behavior, as if some invisible obstacle was blocking their path.

The key to building a high-performing team is to continue to grow, develop, and innovate. Growth and development will help us overcome the stumbling blocks in our way to achievement. It is the foundation of our next step to eliminate the old business mindset that could be wreaking havoc on our life, business, and bottom line. So let's align our mindset with our dreams, mission, purpose, and passion, and learn the tools to unlock the formula for fulfillment and going beyond success!

KEY TAKEAWAYS TO EXECUTE FROM YOUR PURPOSE
- Foresee—Foretell—Forereach.
- Set your Big Hairy Audacious Goal.
- Start with your intention, then commit.
- Design your success: strategic priorities, ideation, assessment, adaptation, alignment, and iteration.
- Get smarter beyond goal setting and implementation: identify everyone's wins and learn how to enroll.
- Create momentum using the dopamine effect.
- Empower and engage.
- Create a high-performing team.

CHAPTER 3

ALIGN YOUR MINDSET

"If my mind can conceive it and my heart can believe it—then I can achieve it."

—MUHAMMAD ALI

Success and happiness are not accidents.

To create a positive change in your leadership and in the collective, you need to develop a positive mindset. That does not mean that you are constantly positive; it just means having the capacity of aligning your mindset to what you want to achieve.

Our mindset is at the origin of our actions. When aligned with our vision, it creates an outstanding momentum for success. A leader's actions, reactions, interactions, perceptions, and choices are most affected by his or her mindset.

I like to define a mindset as the totality of all the neurological and psychological states of mind that we are in—the sum of all our mental activity. Your mindset is the seat of your identity and the most effective way to create change in your leadership.

Since it frames all your experiences, it is important to consider your mindset as foundational to any change you want to create in your life. If your mindset is not aligned with your passion and purpose, you'll have a harder time achieving your goals.

To align your mindset, you need to manage your mind. When you give your mind conflicting information about what you want, it can easily become confused, and you may not get what you want. When you tell your mind, *I want to take my company global, but I don't like to travel*, or, *I want to reach many people, but I don't like talking in front of a crowd about myself or what I'm offering*, or, *I want to expand my business, but I don't want to work long hours*, you are giving your mind mixed signals, which confuses it. Your mind only hears clear and simple instructions.

When you voice a thought and you believe something different, your mind organizes the instruction directly from your *belief*. From the examples above, your mind ignores *I want to grow my business, I want to reach many people, I want to expand my business*, and hears only *I don't like to travel, I don't like talking in front of a crowd*, and *I don't want to work long hours*.

Test it out.

Recall one thing that you've been longing for, but you've never been able to attain. Think of something you have always wanted in your business or in your career, and you could not get. Write it down and check if there is a conflicting belief about it.

Of utmost importance is understanding what you're telling your brain: literally the stories you believe about yourself, consciously or unconsciously, as well the deeply held assumptions you have about your abilities, your relationships, your ambitions, and your behavior, all work together to determine how you leverage your passion and execute from it to realize your ultimate purpose. Whether you realize it or not, your mindset is either your greatest ally in this endeavor or your worst enemy.

Let's do a quick assessment.

STEP 3 QUICK ASSESSMENT: HOW ALIGNED IS YOUR MINDSET?

Rate these statements as true or false from 1–10 on each question. 1 = most false, 10 = most true.

1. I have beliefs about myself that make me never quit and pursue my dream.
2. I often seek feedback from people on what to do and how I can improve.
3. I always strive to understand other people's points of view, and I question my beliefs when they are in conflict with others.
4. I find myself thinking about painful times in the past. When I start feeling bad, I acknowledge my feelings, and I am able to shake these thoughts easily.
5. I am always grateful for the lessons I've learned from my past failures.
6. I am a trusted resource; people seek my opinion, advice, and coaching.
7. I practice a form of meditation, visualization, or mindfulness.
8. I am aware of my core values and beliefs and adhere to them.
9. People consider me to be open-minded and flexible.
10. When I fail at a project, I always take responsibility for my actions.
11. I catch my negative thoughts as they arise and try to change them.

12. I can envision the successful completion of my projects, presentations, and goals before they happen.
13. I have the capacity to transform disempowering thoughts and behaviors into empowering ones.
14. I always bounce back from disappointments and failures with ease.

Your maximum score is 140. The closer you are to 140, the more your mindset is your ally in your personal and professional leadership. As you work through this section, you may want to focus and repeat the exercises where this assessment indicated that you need support. And remember, I recommend that you rate yourself before and after you read this step to measure your progress.

OUR BELIEF MATRIX: THE STORIES WE TELL OURSELVES

It was a particularly frigid and dark winter evening in Montreal. As I was heading to the conference room, my hopes were high for the candidate I was about to interview. Our top executive and second-in-command of the healthcare centers I operated had resigned her position to care for her sick mom. Not only were we losing a top talent, but we were also losing a great leader. She kept our quality of care among the best. She held people accountable and had a very low tolerance for slackers. A hard worker who ruled by what she called "a stick and a carrot," she was both feared and respected by the staff.

It would take an exceptional person to fill her shoes.

But perhaps the woman waiting for me in the conference room on that cold night might just be the one.

The candidate came from a renowned institution and was highly recommended, with great credentials. When I entered the room, I saw our director of human resources talking with a woman in a wheelchair. It was not unusual for our patients to wander into our offices to chat with us. After greeting both women, I turned to my associate and asked if our candidate had arrived.

"My apologies," she said. "I assumed you two had already met. Please meet Mrs. Wilson, the candidate for our executive position."

I confess that I was taken aback because I genuinely thought the person in the wheelchair was a patient of ours.

Now in her late thirties, Martine had earned her MBA with honors from an Ivy League school. Retained by the school as an adjunct professor, she had also been recruited by the firm she had interned for, ultimately working there for almost a decade.

Despite her love for her firm and her admiration for her boss, she was looking for a bigger leadership role. Without me asking, Martine volunteered details about her personal history, describing the accident that killed her father and trapped her, then only four, under the car.

I had interviewed many candidates in my life, but I must admit that Martine was, by far, the most articulate. She was smart and engaging, with a positive outlook and infectious passion for her work. The peace and kindness that emanated from her made me want to learn from her resilience. On paper, her skills and qualifications nearly matched the needs of our organization. Despite lacking the experience of leading an organization the size of ours, I felt compelled to give her a chance.

Martine helped our organization move to great success. She brought with her a state of being-ness that was far more valuable than any set of skills one learns at school or on the job. Almost immediately, I observed a shift in the staff's attitude, as if the team had matured. The managers of the organization reporting to her began developing more efficiency and a spirit of cooperation. They became more responsible, proactive, and willing to take on more duties. They were less reactive to minor setbacks and more focused on what really mattered.

Maybe Martine's presence made them more aware of abilities and privileges they had taken for granted. Her respectful demeanor, positive attitude, and eternal optimism activated in them a willingness to contribute beyond a sense of duty. The unspoken attitude seemed to be: If she can do it, then so can I!

I observed Martine lead and gave her support without micromanaging her. I was always impressed by her positive attitude and the high quality of her work. We gained exponential momentum—a transformative shift in the culture, which celebrated values beyond the financial gains. The business's raison d'être found a deeper meaning in selfless service and contribution to the residents and their families. Employees became more than colleagues, caring for each other like family.

The organization was continuing its journey to greatness until one day, the unthinkable happened: Martine quit. She gave no reason or notice and even refused an exit interview.

I was shocked that she would not even extend us the professional courtesy of helping us ensure the continuity of her job. Having supported and rooted for her, I felt betrayed. More than anything, though, I was confused. What happened?

It would be many years before I got an answer. After my first book was published, Martine reached out to me for professional coaching. I was reluctant at first, but I felt her sincerity and her longing for help. I also hoped that she might explain the conundrum around her abrupt resignation. She needed help with the process of discovering her true self, she told me, and she started our sessions by asking questions about the exercises in the book. She then opened up about the car accident, detailing in full how the accident and her disfigurement affected every aspect of her life, particularly her career. Near tears, she told me she wanted to break through the fears and behavior that kept her stuck professionally.

That's when she finally told me why she quit so abruptly. Back when Martine was working with us, she had a conflict with Nicole, a colleague at work. She had even complained to me about her. Since Nicole had been a loyal member of the team, I coached her, giving her a chance to improve her performance and repair her relationships with her associates. At a company event, Nicole came up to me, hugged me, and publicly expressed her appreciation for what I had done for her.

It turned out that this event triggered Martine, who left soon thereafter. The reasons behind her departure were deeply rooted in her subconscious. After her accident, her mom had quit her job to care for her, leaving her sister with her grandparents, and traveled across the country with Martine to find the best treatment possible. Her mom homeschooled her, protected her, and devoted her undivided attention to what was needed for her condition. Her mom's dedication meant more to Martine than most of us could understand. It was her survival, her sense of identity, and her sense of worth. When I gave equal attention to her co-worker, the same woman Martine had previously voiced concerns about to me, Martine was triggered emotionally. She was rattled to her core. She reacted instinctually, from a survival place of fear, and rather than facing it, she decided to flee. Remembering our previous discussions, I am sure that Martine was not aware of this trigger at the time. Her resignation was a reaction to the angst she felt, the source of which she couldn't identify, and thus could not manage or control.

The mindset that had helped her land and succeed in her dream job was sabotaged by an unseen force that blocked her future development. She was trapped behind an unconscious—and unprocessed—block, which hindered her progress. Unaware of her triggers and blind spots, she became stuck by her own limiting belief.

Like Martine, we all have past hurts buried deep within that cause us to suffer, alone and in silence. They also cause us to judge others and, in doing so, cause them harm.

How many times do we assign meanings to events and start relating to the meaning and not the events?

How many times do we judge people—and limit their ability to prove themselves—by putting them in a box we've created based on our beliefs of them?

When we learn to liberate ourselves from our own past hurts, judgments, beliefs, and meanings, we will feel lighter and freer than we have ever been before—and less likely to judge others. We will find ourselves grounded in the present, no longer living in the past. This may seem like a huge undertaking, but in reality, as we learn to recognize our negative thoughts and start changing them consciously, we start creating a habit which becomes a pattern through repetition. Our brain starts creating a different pathway of thinking which affects our actions and thus creates the intended outcome. I hope that the tools and exercises of this chapter will help you achieve this goal.

Like Martine, our negative narratives consist of our old stories that limit us and thwart our future aspirations. And every one of us has a certain belief about how their life and leadership should be. The meaning that we give our old stories and the "should" of our future stories frame who we become and how we realize our potential.

To achieve becoming the best version of ourselves, however, one of the vital tools we need is to become aware of our own limitations, or what we call the "dream trap."

But, first, we need to take a closer look at how our mindset is established before we're even aware of it.

A blueprint that gives us our life and leadership operating system, our *belief matrix* is our inner software. It's the program behind our skill set that allows us to attain our goals and dreams and succeed. As the main component of our mindset, our belief matrix influences our thoughts, perceptions, meanings, decision-making, actions, reactions, interactions, standards, interpretations, core values, common sense, and problem-solving. Our belief matrix generates our experience and our reality.

How we define success, and the picture we have of it in our mind, will either limit our ability to achieve our goal or propel us toward being truly successful. This is how our mindset creates our reality. It gives us our experiences in life, and it frames our potentialities.

All beliefs originate from this blueprint, which wires our mind and generates what is possible and what is not in our life. Some of our core beliefs are conscious, but many are unconscious. Our mindset determines our perceptions of reality—the positive (*I can lead!*) as well as the negative (*I am not a leader!*) thoughts about ourselves. It is a matrix for our beliefs about success, money, time, entrepreneurship, risk, limitations, narratives, what motivates us, and what is in the way of our success. Our perceptions lead us to a representation of reality that is not the reality itself. We experience things as *we* are and not as *they* are.

All these states of mind are a function of our internal programming and our consciousness about it. They constitute what organizational theorist Peter Senge calls the "invisible soil" of our mindset. In an interview, Senge posed this question to MIT's Otto Scharmer: "What if the quality of the visible socioeconomic outcomes is a function of the invisible social soil that resides in the blind spot of our perception?"[4]

The same question can be asked regarding leadership: What if the quality of our leadership outcomes is a function of the invisible soil of our mindset?

Dwelling in this invisible soil are all of our learnings and experiences, and the reasons behind our behaviors, attitudes, and choices. It is the host of our beliefs about ourselves—about success/failure, abundance/scarcity, money/wealth, time, health, wellness, and more.

---

4 Otto Scharmer, *The Essentials of Theory U: Core Principles and Applications* (Oakland, CA: Berrett-Koehler Publishers, 2018), 62.

Our beliefs and thoughts create our reality and the world around us. They are the origin of our actions. Our beliefs create our actions, and our actions create our patterns of behavior. By acting on our inner beliefs about our own leadership, we can change how we express our leadership in the world. The fact is, we have a choice.

When we are young, our minds are vulnerable and easily influenced by our parents, or those who raised us, and what they show us through their words and their actions. We emulate some of their behaviors, and act like them at times, without having developed the capacity to understand our behaviors. We are like sponges receiving raw data as true, without any capacity to edit, sort, or select this information; therefore, it imprints us deeply.

We believe the information even more than our parents, who might not even be conscious of what they're delivering. We mirror their positive or negative thoughts and emulate their positive or negative behaviors without discernment. When you were a child, you certainly learned different behaviors. Your parents rewarded certain behaviors and punished others. You learned very young what was acceptable and what was not and what you needed to do to win your parents' love and attention. This was passed on to them by their parents. So on and so forth. This is how some of our family values become ingrained in us, making them so hard to break. This is at the origin of our core values because as children, we regard our parents as our Gods and whatever we learn from them is sacred. What is acceptable or not acceptable was passed on to you by the people closest to you—your parents, extended family, friends, teachers, and community.

Some of these beliefs you'll no doubt recognize; others will be unconscious. You may realize that your low tolerance for anyone who shows up late for an interview—even if he has a legitimate reason—comes from the importance your parents placed on being on time. And that his tardiness was an important factor in not being called back for a second interview. If wearing red lipstick was not acceptable to your mom, chances are a candidate showing up with it on will subconsciously trigger irritation in you.

Our beliefs are formed by what we learn; they are shaped by our experiences early on and by what we interpreted those experiences to mean. Our personal, unique experiences make our belief systems unique. For the purpose of our work, I would like to distinguish two types of Core Beliefs:

1. Those we have formed about ourselves.
2. Those we have formed about everybody and everything else.

The first ones are created either because of the conviction we have about ourselves or because we've bought into someone else's belief about us and internalized it. They can also emerge not only from our childhood experiences, but in our experiences of success, failure, and how others perceive us.

The second set of beliefs is influenced by how our beliefs about ourselves fit or clash with our environments, our communities, our culture, and the media. The biases we acquire from the environment, the beliefs of our family members or the people who raised us, schoolteachers, childhood friends, our religious communities, our culture, and the media.

In reality, each set of beliefs informs the other, and, together, they form our Belief Matrix.

As we store information and form new beliefs, our belief matrix becomes our main filter for perception. We keep any information that agrees with our beliefs because it is familiar and affirms our way of seeing the world. We reject any thought, idea, or proposal that does not agree with our beliefs. The thought that comes through is filtered according to the following criteria:

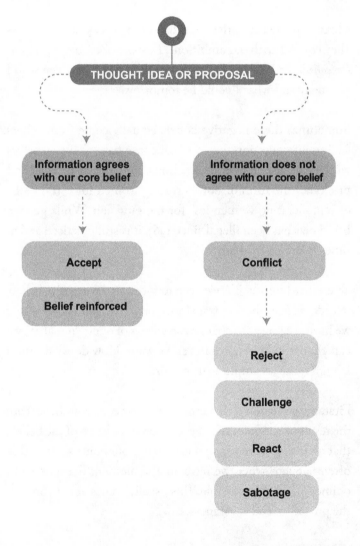

Our core beliefs could be conscious or unconscious, influenced by the cultural environment in which we live and work. The positive ones move us forward *(I am capable of successfully executing complex ideas. I am a strong, compassionate leader who helps others fulfill their mission).* The positive ones also propel us towards success and happiness.

Meanwhile, the negative ones limit our success and progress. They conflict with our ambition. *(I want to lead this project, but I'm convinced I'll fail.)* They create a disconnect between who I am today and what I could be tomorrow.

Sometimes these negative beliefs actually come from others, calling into question the core beliefs we have about ourselves, which can disempower our actions. Sometimes our cultural bias takes the form of not recruiting women for certain jobs or remunerating women less for the same job. While gender-based bias has been illegal since 1963, it is still practiced and at times tolerated by many.

To create a limitless life, we need to focus on the negative beliefs in order to learn how to transform them. The good news is that we have the power to change the wiring of our own matrix; we can choose to believe whatever we want. How do we do that? It's not quite as simple as it sounds.

First, the good news. Remember that our conscious beliefs are the result of our point of view, so in order to let go of the beliefs that no longer serve us, we must change our point of view. This often happens when we have an aha moment that alters our opinion of what is possible. This usually comes about through the process of self-awareness.

The not-so-good news is that our unconscious beliefs are programmed deep in our cellular memory, hidden from our conscious mind, which makes them difficult to access. The limiting ones may very well be in conflict with what we want to achieve and sabotage our efforts, setting up a conflict between our goal and our ability to attain it. Because the mind can't hold conflicting beliefs, it will default to the familiar and reject the unfamiliar. It limits our leadership expansion and fulfillment of our potential.

Even though our mind knows how to do certain things, we don't always succeed. Our unconscious beliefs are at play behind the scenes, affecting the outcome. For instance, we all have big New Year's resolution plans: we want to get fit, exercise, eat healthy, carve out time for relaxation, etc. We know how to get there, yet we don't always succeed. Often that's because our unconscious mind isn't on board. It is constantly reminding us that we don't deserve time off, we haven't achieved enough yet, and on and on.

There are two major culprits that have perfected the art of limiting our success: the belief that we are not good enough, and the belief that we are a victim.

The first one is a hindrance to pursuing our dreams, and the second is an impediment to accepting responsibility and accountability—two major characteristics of success and excellence. Together, these two culprits serve as the origin of our limiting beliefs.

For many, limiting beliefs stem from an impactful event in their life. The nagging, critical voice that keeps the internal dialogue going inside of you is nothing more than a limiting belief you hold about yourself, such as, *I am not capable enough*, *I am not good enough*, *I cannot make it on my own*, or *I am not lovable enough*.

The belief of not being good enough hijacks our mindset and creates our reality. The number one reason that most of us get discouraged from pursuing our dream is this negative little voice telling us, *I can't do it*, *There's no way I can start a business*, *No one would ever hire me as a CEO*, *I have nothing valuable to contribute*, *I can't close a deal*, and so on and so forth.

Erik Erikson, a developmental psychologist whose influential theories of psychosocial development, maintained that personality develops in a predetermined order. During each stage, the person experiences what he called "an identity crisis," which could impact them positively or negatively. Usually, the crisis is of a psychosocial nature, a stressful experience where we believe that someone or some set of circumstances has let us down. We feel victimized and become disillusioned with the world and start adopting a new survival strategy. This strategy could be positive (if we manage to learn the lesson), or this strategy could limit our potential (if we get stuck in its negative story).

At some point in our lives, we likely decided that we were not good enough. Now that has impacted us professionally, because the fear of others discovering what we already "know" about ourselves threatens our ability to succeed.

Our inner program starts avoiding situations that could generate a similar feeling. Our decisions are determined by our previous experience, and our impact becomes a function of our past and not of the infinite future possibilities. We are on autopilot. Our patterns of behavior have become ingrained in our subconscious-conditioned mind, and we can't free ourselves. That's why it's often much easier for us to anticipate other people's behavior than it is to anticipate our own, predicting their response while being oblivious to our own.

The wounds from our childhood are at the origin of our fears, which prevent us from growing and force us to develop defense mechanisms. They create a barrier that limits our leadership potential, and they impact the decisions we make. The traumas of long ago keep us feeling insecure, or unsafe, when we're faced with situations that trigger a flight or fight response. These past wounds can also block our flow of energy, and disconnect us from our purpose and our future.

If we shed light on some of our past wounds—from failure at a project in our adulthood to the failure of being in our childhood—and start healing them, we can begin to remove the roadblocks that prevent us from responding as a conscious leader. We start exploring new ways of being that we would not have discovered otherwise.

This unconscious process affects your mindset. As long as you stay stuck thinking the same thoughts, you perform the same actions and are affected by the same emotional triggers. Consequently, your life cannot change. By creating the same mental activity, you create the same outcome, and your future is a continuation of your past. The author Dr. Joe Dispenza describes it this way:

By staying in the known—following the same sequence each

day of thinking the same thoughts, making the same choices, demonstrating the same programmed habits, recreating the same experiences that stamp the same networks of neurons into the same patterns to reaffirm the same familiar feeling called *you*— you are repeating the same level of mind over and over again. In time, your brain becomes automatically programmed to do any one of those sequences more easily and effortlessly the next time, and then the next time, and so on.[5]

Some dysfunctions burn through from one generation to another like wildfire until one person in a given generation has the courage to face the pattern, bring awareness to it in their own family, and commit to changing it. When the change happens, the person interrupts the cycle, leverages the wisdom of their past learnings, brings peace to their ancestors, and spares their children from a never-ending cycle.

In his early childhood, Dr. Martin Luther King, Jr., became friends with a white neighbor whose father owned a business. When the boys were about six years old, they started school. Dr. King attended a school for black children, while his close friend attended a whites-only school. The parents of the white boy forbade their son to play with Dr. King, because he was black. Dr. King's first reaction was to hate every white person. Yet, through self-awareness, he was able to transform his stand, and took his courage into his hands to change a dysfunctional cycle for generations to come.

We are not interested in changing the positives of generational cultures, but the stubborn cultural neuroses that continue to haunt us generation after generation. Once we heal from the

---

5   Joe Dispenza, *Becoming Supernatural: How Common People Are Doing the Uncommon* (Carslbad, CA: Hay House, 2017), p 126.

negativity of generational cultures, we can make room for the positives to grow for future generations. When we heal those neuroses and expand the positives, we heal the suffering of future generations.

While the dysfunction in our mind that originated from an experience earlier in life can explain how our mind gets wired to limit us, it also gives us hope. By becoming aware of those roadblocks, we take the first step toward reprogramming our mind for a better future.

The second core belief—that we are always the victim—could be a result of a decision we made earlier in life, or simply a learned behavior from the dysfunctional attitude of the people who raised us. No matter how horrible the events of your life may have been—or have become—if you are not able to shift your consciousness from victimhood to mastery, you'll remain imprisoned by your self-destructive beliefs, unable to reclaim your true self. It takes tremendous strength and courage to make this shift—especially during very challenging situations. If you are dealing with a crisis at work or a betrayal by someone you trusted, or an unexpected legal or financial crisis, it is natural to ask yourself, *Why me?* But if you dwell there too long, you will come to believe in your victimhood, and then you won't be able to get out of it.

In victim consciousness, we are not able or willing to let others in; therefore, there is no possibility for growth. If we feel like victims, we will only dwell in self-pity and try to get people to sympathize with us. We will revisit our stories repeatedly as we try to use them to get sympathy from others, and rally them around our point of view. It's exhausting for others to be around us when we're suffering from the "poor-me" syndrome.

As humans, we naturally strive to make meaning out of our experiences; as victims, we get obsessed with creating meaning out of what we believe has happened *to* us. We may have even forgotten the actual cause of our grudges, but that doesn't stop us from harboring them and holding on to feelings of "poor me."

When we *behave* like a victim of events, people, or circumstances, *being* a victim becomes our identity. Our energy gets consumed by explaining and justifying our position, instead of being proactive, taking charge, and making things happen. Victimhood has zapped our passion, causing us to question our purpose and our ability to achieve our goals. Our mindset becomes a jail we seem unable to escape from, which leads us to believe that we aren't worthy of success or capable of realizing our untapped potential. Releasing yourself from victimhood is a critical step toward becoming responsible—for your own work and, if you're a manager, for the work of others. It increases the level of accountability and functionality in the work environment. Just as positive thoughts and positive feelings can promote a positive work environment, negative thoughts and negative emotions like victimization, resentment, anger, and frustration can keep you from realizing your goals and vision.

It's difficult to see that connection, however, because these negative reactions can remain hidden in your inner programming until you're forced to pay attention to them. Of course, you won't notice them all at once, nor should you. It's more like peeling back an onion, one layer at a time, one belief at a time. Remember, though, if you continue to push them aside, you can affect not only the outcome but the process as well—the *way* you show up for yourself and others.

The good news is once you do notice them, you have the opportunity to transform them from limiting beliefs to empowering ones. In doing so, you become a more conscious and effective leader.

How, then, do we escape the "program" that we unknowingly are trapped in through a lifetime of social conditioning and many lifetimes of unconscious programming? Programming happens all the time in our life, not only during our childhood years. But those of us who have the courage to go back to those painful early experiences and make peace with them have the key to accessing "beingness" in life from an authentic place. Our actions become more factual, and we can tame our reactions. We can pinpoint some of the unconscious triggers that are hidden from our view. Therefore, our behavior is no longer given to us by the past. Should we become connected to a future possibility, our actions can be given to us from that potentiality. We become much happier and more fulfilled in our life.

Our life is a series of narratives. At times, I think that our life is a story. Think about it. The way we describe our life is based on a tale. Martine was telling a specific story about her life, centered around her accident. Unconsciously, everything radiated from this story, every decision, every relationship, every type of behavior.

When we feel bad about our life, we get into a repetitive loop of thoughts that describes the sequence of events and cements our belief that we're no good. It's like we're the tragic figure—and the director—in our own movie. We are even addicted to that storyline, to the way it makes us feel, even if the feeling is negative. Our story of who we are is based on a perception of who we became because of our past successes and failures.

One thing is sure: we perpetuate our life because of our narratives. If these stories are positive and joyful, we continue creating the same: success breeds success. If these narratives are negative, we also continue to keep them alive *and* the longer we do that, the harder it becomes to break through and change our life's course. To change and create a new path, we must create a new account or a new narrative of the events so that we can change our future. Otherwise, our history will continue to determine our present and future.

The reason why our past failures keep us constrained is that we don't change the narrative about them. Therefore, if you want to change your life and your leadership, change your relationship with your past failures and learn how to leverage them. To leverage your past failures, you must reframe your narratives in a positive way. For example:

Despite the loss that I have incurred, I am grateful that I still have my business and my products have improved. I honor my experience, I acknowledge what I've learned from it, and I vow to make it a guide for creating a positive social impact.

EXERCISE: TELL YOUR STORY.

Step 1.

Write your life story in three sentences: one sentence about your past, one about your present, and one about your future.

Step 2.

What similarities do you notice between your past and present? Is there a similar pattern between the past and the present? Write it down.

Step 3.

Describe something good that you learned from your story.

Step 4.

Write down one positive thing that your story revealed about you. Read your answers aloud.

Step 5.

How would you use your story to empower your leadership?

REPROGRAM YOUR MINDSET FOR SUCCESS

One of my earliest professional failures occurred during my very first job, as assistant director of the American University Hospital of Beirut. With no leadership experience under my belt, I was responsible for, among other things, the ancillary medical services of the hospital. One of my assignments was to reorganize the medical records department, as the hospital was experiencing a huge backlog in processing patients' discharge summaries.

The problem was that the physicians were not signing the discharge plans, so the department could not process them. Back then, the department was not automated the way it is today. The accumulation of unsigned medical records created a bottleneck in many departments, including billing, quality assurance, and outpatient follow-ups.

Fixing this was one of the first assignments for a job "beyond my wildest dreams." I took my task very seriously, determined to prove that I could do it. In the infinite wisdom of a twenty-three-year-old graduate, I decided to take the bull by the horns by sending a letter to all the physicians who were not responding to the pleas from the medical records department, threatening to suspend their admitting privileges if their discharge summaries were not signed by a certain date.

Although the medical records department started to improve their processing, I noticed that some doctors were avoiding me: they didn't confirm committee meetings or simply didn't show up; they didn't return my calls even when I befriended their assistants.

No physician had their admitting privileges suspended, and yet I felt a certain tension around me. I noticed that the medical records director was visiting the director of the hospital more often than me, even though she reported to me. While the results of my first task were clearly heading in the right direction, my popularity had dwindled among my supporters, including the hospital director.

I decided to schedule a meeting with him and ask for feedback. When we met, he casually mentioned he had retracted my memo, the day after I had sent it.

My embarrassment was beyond description, and my anxiety started to build up. My fear kicked in, and I was facing my fear of failure head-on. I wanted to flee my office, go home, and never come back. I wanted to apologize for not clearing the letter with the director before sending it. But none of that happened. Luckily, the director had a meeting to go to, which provided the perfect outlet for both of us. It was as uncomfortable for him as it was for me. I retreated to my office, embarrassed of my failure, and got busy creating possible scenarios in my mind.

If I tell you that this was the most valuable lesson I have ever learned in my years of leadership, would you believe me?

Here's why it was: I learned to take the time to assess every task thoroughly before acting, and to recognize the power players in each institution and how to engage them. I learned that making people do what you want by fear or threat never works. Instead, motivating people and enrolling them in their own benefits will empower them (and me) and yield the intended outcome. I also learned about respect and diplomacy.

I learned, also, to forgive myself, and to forgive the director for not telling me about my mistake or giving me the opportunity to correct it.

Perhaps most importantly, I learned how to reprogram my mindset from one of fear of failure, to a more positive mindset of the opportunity to succeed.

In many instances, the lessons we learn from our mistakes far outweigh our actual failures. By revisiting our past failures, we approach them with the intention of extracting their benefits. By reframing those experiences, we can switch our mindset from negative to positive and even become grateful for the experience. Without the failure I experienced, I would not have been the successful entrepreneur and leader I became.

In this section, you will learn five important tools to reprogram your mind for ultimate success as you endeavor to align it with your vision.

Reprogram your Mindset for Success

01 Reframe your narratives

Recognize signals of a dream trap **02**

03 Interrupt your habitual mind

Turn around your negative thought **04**

05 Switch your language

TOOL #1. REFRAME YOUR NARRATIVES.

Sometimes, to reframe our story, we need to revisit it. We are all silently suffering from past hurts buried deep within our beings. In this section, we will go through a powerful technique to liberate ourselves from past hurts, and transform our experience into a catalyst for positive change.

 It is not unusual to believe that the best way to "move on" is to put the story behind us and never think about it again. However, although we may push it as far back in the past as possible, we can never erase it. We can't heal what we refuse to acknowledge. Unfortunately, the adage is true: *What you can't be with can't let you be!*

There are feelings and beliefs associated with your story that are alive and can be triggered by an occurrence or an emotion that reminds you of your original trauma. That is why the best way I have found to deal with my own story is to relive it, release the encapsulated emotional pain, and bring into light the lessons my story has taught me. I know it can be frightening at first, but the benefit of leveraging your past will outweigh the discomfort of this exercise. Regardless of how significant or trivial your story is, the meaning that you gave it can make you feel helpless and victimized.

We are not to be judged or blamed for our stories. Instead, we should be measured by the awareness we need to consciously realize how our stories impact our life. Of course, these stories impact our immediate family—children, wife, husband, and siblings—as well as our friends and communities. They also affect our ability to succeed as a leader. For this work, we will focus on a leadership failure. Such an experience can limit you to a certain mindset, which modulates your actions, and prevents you from believing you can take on similar projects without the fear of failure. To break through all of this, you will need to reframe your story instead of being framed by it.

So, how can we escape from the negative impact our story has on our life, minimize the impact that it has on others, and commit to writing a new narrative?

The key is to take the *learning* not the failure from your story and to take that learning into a future endeavor. My story illustrates this point.

Our eagerness to take on challenges or shy away from new responsibilities is often associated with our fear of failure. This fear is what can stand in the way of our greatness.

How do you feel about failure? We are all afraid to fail at any undertaking. For some of us, this fear is crippling enough to make us shy away from projects. I had a friend who spent his life micromanaging everything, from his colleagues to his subordinates, his bosses, his family, and his friends. He went as far as creating a process for how to wash his strawberries. Do you recall a person like that on your team who stands over you, noting all the bits and pieces of a project as you're working on it? Or an assistant who needs hand holding about each decision, little or big, until you end up doing it yourself instead of delegating the project to her? At the root of all these patterns of behavior is the fear of failure.

When we learn to respond to failures in new and empowering ways, we literally change our relationship to success. When we learn to embrace failures and realize that what we call failures are not really failures, but approaches we've tried in the past that did not yield the intended outcome, we can change that approach. At the same time, we can give thanks to the initial approaches for teaching us the lessons we needed to learn from these experiences. This is the basis for reframing your narratives: you learn to embrace your past failures, extracting the wisdom within them and starting to feel gratitude for what you've learned.

Success, then, becomes an ongoing process. Redefining failure helps us to succeed more often: our failures become steps towards success. Success and failure come together, and they are equally beneficial.

What do you do when you want to leverage an investment? In simple words, the profits made from the investment become greater than the payable interest. To leverage your failures means to use the failures to maximize success. Go back to each failure, and extract the lessons it can teach you. This step may be painful, because your feelings may still be raw from the experience. The more painful your failure, the more important it is to go back and revisit it. Accepting what happened and acknowledging your feelings about what happened is the first step of transformation. Leveraging your experience will necessitate extracting all the positives from it, even if these are not apparent to you.

Failures and breakdowns will tend to repeat themselves until we learn from them and change our narrative about them. In the previous exercise, you may have noticed similarities between the past and the present. The key to changing your future is to change your narrative about the present. Your future is either a continuation of the past or a new creation from the future.

You can complete the exercise below to leverage your failures and reframe your narrative about your failure so that you can create a successful future.

EXERCISE: REFRAME YOUR NARRATIVE ABOUT YOUR FAILURE, LEVERAGE THE LESSON TO EMPOWER YOUR FUTURE.

Step 1.

Choose a time when you feel you really bombed. Now create three columns: the failure story, the impact of the failure, and the learnings from the failure. Make sure to list everything that comes to your mind in order of occurrence. It is best if you don't edit yourself and don't judge yourself. Just list them as facts.

LIST OF FAILURES	IMPACT OF FAILURE	LESSON LEARNED

Step 2.

Describe a situation in which you were able to accept and acknowledge how your failure impacted you and others within your organization. Write it down.

Step 3.

Now, write down what lessons you are grateful for that came out of your failure story.

Step 4.

Next, reframe your story about your failure, writing a new narrative in three sentences: one about the past, one about the present, and one about the future.

Example:

LIST OF FAILURES	IMPACT OF FAILURE	LESSON LEARNED
Assess and diagnose the power dynamics at the hospital before I sent my note to the physicians.	Alienation of physicians Resignation of a surgeon The letter sent by my director The impression of how I occurred to my team The time to recover from the fallout	Assess and diagnose each situation before acting. Take dynamics and power play into consideration. Making people do what you want and managing by fear is worthless. Enrolling the team in their own benefits will empower them far more than managing by force.

New Narrative: In the past, I failed my first project because I acted too quickly. At present, I fully assess a project at hand prior to execution. I envision success from the future, and love enrolling and empowering my teams on their way to achieving their goal.

You can apply this tool to any negative story you have, big or small. When you define the facts of your story, you are not minimizing what happened. Rather, you are simply taking what worked and leaving behind what didn't. You stop identifying with the failure, let go of the fear, and embrace the belief that you can turn the lessons you've learned toward a similar project. You're turning your past failure into a future success. It's not unlike a little kid who is trying to ride a bicycle for the first time and keeps falling. He feels like a failure; he'll *never* be able to do it. In fact, he's terrified of getting back on the bike. Instead of taking the bike away from him and giving him back his tricycle, his mom talks to him about his fears, they figure out what worked and what didn't, and then devise a plan to try again—with success.

In sharing your new narrative, make sure to incorporate your experience of failure in a positive light. Don't bypass the lessons you've learned. You need to believe in your narrative before sharing it.

Have you ever heard this expression: *Tell me your story, and I will tell you who you are*? I don't agree with this statement because your story does not have to determine who you are, but the *way* you live it and share it will.

TOOL #2. RECOGNIZE SIGNALS OF A DREAM TRAP, AND INTERRUPT THE CYCLE TO GET OUT OF A RUT.

A dream trap is when you keep repeating the same actions and getting the same results while hoping that your dream comes true, but it never does. When your "yesterdays" become your "tomorrows," when you're stuck spinning your wheels, and your goals have become unattainable, the reality is that your dream is trapped. You may be dissatisfied, unmotivated, and settling for a job that is not fulfilling. And to top it off, as a result, no one is taking your dream seriously.

Sometimes you can get caught up in conflicting thoughts about yourself, your business, and what you should or shouldn't do.

That's a signal that you're trapped in a dysfunctional mind-set, which is preventing you from confidently moving forward. When you keep doing the same thing and expecting different results, it's time to shake up your habitual mind.

Do you feel at times that you have a project within you waiting to happen, and your little negative inner voice is preventing you from starting it?

The fact that you don't see the car in the side mirror doesn't mean it's not there. If you don't use another mechanism of checking over your shoulder, you risk a crash. In the same way, even if you are unaware of your limiting thoughts, beliefs, behaviors, and patterns, they can still affect your decision-making process, your business choices, your future, and the future of your family, team, community, and society.

It's rarely easy to identify our negative beliefs—they so often hide in the blind spots of our perceptions—but it *is* possible to learn how to catch their signals.

So how do we transform them, align back with our dream, and create our future on our own terms?

The key is to go back to your mission statement, vision, passion, and purpose. You may have not even noticed that you became stuck in a rut. Re-examine your personal goal and check if it is still relevant. If so, acknowledge that you got stuck in a routine that did not help you move towards your goals. Go back to Step 2, and design your success by applying the framework for fulfilling strategies and goals. Start small, and don't forget to reward yourself each step of the way!

TOOL #3. INTERRUPT YOUR HABITUAL MIND.

Our habitual mind is the ruminating mind, which tends to think the same thoughts that keep repeating and repeating themselves. At times we keep thinking the same thoughts, hoping for more understanding or insights. Many perfectionists have a tendency to keep thinking and analyzing a situation to get it perfect, but the cycle will throw you in a downhill spiral. Thoughts create. They are behind our actions. Repeating the same negative thoughts over and over again will keep you stuck in that old rut and even, at times, take the wrong action.

Left to its own devices, a habitual mind can become restless, unsettled, and uncontrollable, living up to its nickname—the Monkey Mind. Uninterrupted, the habitual mind gets stuck on automatic and will keep creating a future that resembles the past. You will have a hard time imagining a future of possibilities, or believing in your ability to manifest it.

Our automatic mind is much more familiar with thoughts that judge and compare. For example: *This is good for me,* or *This is bad for me*; *I should do this,* or *I should shy away from that*; *She is better than I am,* or *she does not have the courage*; *I am incompetent,* or *I am great.* And on it goes. These comparisons and judgments either originate from a belief or coalesce into one.

Our habitual mind ruminates on negative thoughts about a future through worries and anxiety that are unfounded, pessimistic, and unlikely to occur. Our mind is also a conduit for great thoughts to emerge. For that to happen, we first need to interrupt and neutralize the negative ones.

It's time to take a hard look not only at your actions, but also at the thought processes and reasons behind those actions. What's playing in the background? It's your habitual mind.

The easiest way to interrupt our habitual mind is to catch the negative thoughts that come from fear, friction, restriction, or unease. Then, label them, challenge them, and turn them around. You have to cut through the patterns of your habitual mind if you want to change your actions and change the outcome, question your negative thoughts, and move your action forward as you enhance your self-esteem.

EXERCISE: QUESTION YOUR REPETITIVE THOUGHT AND MOVE IT FORWARD.

When you catch yourself almost obsessing about a negative thought, follow these steps:

Step 1.

Distinguish if the thought is coming from fear or it is a fact.

Stop and ask yourself the question: Is that thought 100% accurate? Is it a fact? Did it already happen or a fear waiting to happen?

Step 2.

How could you improve on what has already happened, or prevent the troubling thought from occurring if it did not happen?

Step 3.

Create a small action towards improving on it. If it has happened, think of a small correction: for example, an apology or a stop-gap action. If you do not have much say in the matter, try to brainstorm a reversal action or a protective one. For instance, if you are afraid that the company will eliminate your position, think of the skills that you have or that you can develop for another position, start working on your resumé, etc.

Step 4.

Make it happen today!

Execute the small action. This will help you enhance your self-esteem and interrupt the cycle of the ruminating mind.

Now you can move to tool #4 to turn around your negative thoughts.

TOOL #4. TURN AROUND YOUR NEGATIVE THOUGHTS.

Every time you feel the impulse or catch yourself with a negative or conflicting thought about yourself and your business, stop and challenge it. Ask yourself, *Is this a belief coming from the past or is it a response to the present? Is this a belief you always default to?*

Every time I hit a wall in my career, I found that what was keeping me stuck was either my Monkey Mind or my narrative about the past. Either I had a conflicting thought about whether I could achieve a goal or a negative thought that prevented me from going to the next level. And I could not let it go. It threatened to derail my passion for growth and my determination to succeed. I had to find a way to interrupt the pattern of negativity, and catch the signals early enough to transform it. So, this is what I did. I first noticed the thought that was getting in my way. I labeled it as a form of resistance. I decided to see it and chose to do the opposite. In this way, the resistance became the catalyst for growth and for the creation of a new pathway in my brain. This pathway became a pattern for success through repetition.

I remember when I was asked to create the one-day surgery clinic at the American Hospital of Paris. My initial reaction was that I lacked experience. Didn't the CEO already know that? The concept was new, and my fear of failure took hold of me, because it was my first job in Paris, where we had moved just a few months back. My Monkey Mind went to town, listing all the reasons—over and over and over again—why I could not do it. I felt comfortable declining the project. And then... just as I was about to render my decision to the CEO, I asked myself the question, *What if I fail?* The answer came to me: *I would develop new skills.* The little voice inside kept at it: *But you can't do it! You don't know the system or the physicians or the culture.* This argument continued until I decided to stop, name, and feel the emotions behind the argument, which allowed me to calm my inner voice and do exactly the opposite.

EXERCISE: TURN AROUND YOUR NEGATIVE THOUGHTS.

Step 1.

Sit quietly and move into a state of relaxation by taking a few deep breaths.

Step 2.

Stop and look at some situation or area in your professional or personal life where you keep meeting resistance or getting the same results. This could vary from a position that you keep recruiting for with different versions of people who do not stick around, or the different relationships that keep "not working out" in your life.

Step 3.

Take a moment and write down the first situation that comes to mind. If nothing does, think of a recent decision made at your business—not by you, but by someone else—that irritated you, and write down the first one that comes to your mind.

Step 4.

What is your opinion about that situation or decision? Write it down.

Step 5.

What is the core belief, principle, or core value around your opinion? Write it down.

Step 6.

Describe your belief. Could you trace how you formulated your belief? Is it because of an experience or a meaning you gave to an experience? Is it because you learned it this way? Do you know who influenced your belief? Is it a core belief about yourself or a belief about how things should be done?

Step 7.

How has this belief affected your ability to succeed?

Step 8.

Imagine yourself without this belief. What would happen in your life if you did not have this belief?

Step 9.

What is the impact that your belief had on your life and on others at work, at home, in your family, and in your community?

Step 10.

Are you ready to give it up or upgrade it?

Step 11.

Turn the belief around and address your concern.

Example: *I want to create my own business, but if I do, I can't spend enough time with my family.* Instead, ask the question, "How can creating my own business allow me to spend more time with my family?" Many ideas could bridge the gap and reconcile the two goals. For instance, making more income may allow you to hire some help with the chores around the house. You can then turn around this thought and work on this inner conflict.

Write down the turnaround belief and the goals to achieve.

Step 12.

Visualize your desired outcome, and intensify the image you want to create.

Turning around your negative thoughts is a continuous effort, like catching a thief who tries to sneak into your house first through the door and then through every window he can find. We have to stay alert to the signals we're receiving from our thoughts, our language, and our state of mind that keep us from moving forward, and then use tools to interrupt them. When there is friction in the mind, we need to pause, listen, and examine what's behind it.

TOOL #5. SWITCH YOUR LANGUAGE.

How many times a day do we witness ideas killed by phrases such as *Based on my experience, this will not work!* or *But we've always done it this way! Why should we change?*

Judgments like this limit our ability to imagine the future and create a new vision, especially when they are verbalized by those who are charged with leading the team. Sometimes it is easier to become aware of and change the language we use than it is to acknowledge and change the beliefs we hold, for the simple reason that words are easy to spot in a conversation. As soon as we become aware that the language we are using is affecting the success of a project, it becomes imperative that we change our vocabulary before it can irrevocably damage the outcome.

We can change course by switching from "This project will never get off the ground. I can't believe we're still doing this" to "We can do this, let's come together, assess, and make it happen!" Not only do you empower others with your words, but you are also effectively silencing the doubts from your own Monkey Mind, choosing success over failure.

Ensuring that your inner language and your outer language align with your passion and your purpose is about programming your brain and your mindset for success. You can choose to be in control by consciously directing your awareness towards what you desire, then setting aside any thought that conflicts with that. Are the words you speak positive or negative? Are you talking yourself into failure? Is your negative self-talk letting you down? Are all your ideas expressed in the positive and not the negative?

Cynthia, one of my directors, believed that she could make seemingly impossible tasks happen. I can say without hesitation that I never saw her fail. Her confident language reflected the command of her position. When she spoke, everyone working with her knew she was going to deliver on her promise. And everyone responded to her positivity in kind.

On the other hand, another director, Joe, regularly questioned his strategic vision and doubted his ability to deliver. I remember he had been working on the launch of a year-long, million-dollar project. In the first month, he was confident and excited about his strategy, and he was able to rally his team. But when his expenses increased over the next several months before getting a return, he started to question his approach. It was expected not to see the return over investment this early in the project, but his hesitation about the future robbed him from sustaining a vision of success. I'm sure you can guess what happened next—his plan stalled. While it wasn't a total failure, it didn't produce the results anyone wanted, and he slowly but surely lost the confidence of his team and, even worse, many of his team members asked to move to other projects. In the end, he was not able to enroll his team in a vision he himself didn't believe in.

Why is that? Because he saw the lack of revenues in the first six months as a reflection of his failure to be a good project manager. Rather than championing his small victories and ability to manage setbacks, he only communicated the project's setbacks and dead ends. His language was rooted in failure and disappointment because he couldn't interrupt his habitual mind. He was unable to challenge the obstinate thoughts that were limiting his ability to deliver something that he was perfectly capable of delivering.

The key is to foster a mindset like Cynthia and interrupt the mindset that sabotaged Joe.

Applying these techniques and repeating them will bring about gradual changes. The answer is to practice and persevere. Repetition is crucial for any mind-programming success, because it imprints your desired outcomes rather than falling victim to negative thoughts about fear and failure.

Now, congratulations on completing the most challenging and rewarding section of this book. Mastering your mindset will generate rewards beyond your wildest dreams. It will make you limitless in attaining your vision and ambition. With repetition and practice of these steps, making them routine, you will be surprised at your own achievements. Your success will surpass your expectations. Give yourself a pat on the back, and believe in yourself!

KEY TAKEAWAYS TO ALIGN YOUR MINDSET

- Your belief matrix is made of two types of Core Beliefs: those you have formed about yourself, and those you have formed about everybody and everything else. Your core beliefs could be conscious or unconscious.
- Reprogram your Mindset for success. Your negative beliefs about yourself could determine your future which becomes a function of your past and not of the infinite future possibilities.
- Reframe your narratives. By reframing failure experiences, you can switch your mindset from negative to positive.
- Recognize signals of a dream trap. When your "yesterdays" become your "tomorrows," when you're stuck spinning your wheels, and your goals have become unattainable, the reality is that your dream is trapped.
- Interrupt your habitual mind. The easiest way to interrupt your habitual mind is to catch the negative thoughts that come from fear, friction, restriction, or unease, label them, challenge them, and turn them around.
- Turn around your negative thoughts. It is a continuous effort, like catching a thief who is constantly trying to sneak in. When you do, turn him around.
- Switch your language. Ensure that your inner language and your outer language align with your passion and your purpose. This programs your brain and your mindset for success.

CHAPTER 4

PROGRAM YOUR EMOTIONS

"Great leaders move us. They ignite our passion and inspire the best in us. When we try to explain why they are so effective, we speak of strategy, vision, or powerful ideas. But the reality is much more primal: Great leadership works through emotions."

—DANIEL GOLEMAN, RICHARD BOYATZIS, ANNIE MCKEE[6]

Twenty-some years ago, this statement would have been vilified by many leaders who believed that leadership was singularly about skills, ability, and knowledge. Thanks to Daniel Goleman, Richard Boyatzis, Annie McKee, and many others who led the emotional intelligence movement, however, today almost every big organization uses emotional competency testing or language in their recruitment.

For my work, I use the emotions and the momentum they

---

6   Daniel Goleman, Richard Boyatzis, and Annie McKee, *Primal Leadership: Unleashing the Power of Emotional Intelligence* (Brighton, MA: Harvard Business Review Press, 2013), p. 3.

create to program, align, and manifest our passion, vision, goals, and mission in leadership and in life.

The process of aligning your mindset, however, can't be complete without the ability to program your emotions. What I mean by programming them is: understanding them, knowing how to process them, preempting the triggers as you become aware of them, releasing the negative ones and directing the positive ones to power up your end goal. The tools and exercises in this chapter will help you do so, to consciously embody your purpose and mission—and manifest your intention in the world. Emotions play a fundamental role in our mindset. Cognitive research has shown that even experts' decisions are, at times, biased by unrelated emotions. If our emotional considerations are compromised, our reasoning and logic also become flawed. Conversely, when we are aware of our emotions and know how to direct them and use them, the path to our best life becomes clear.

We learn how to:

- Reduce our reactivity and respond to unadulterated facts, which will access our emotional triggers in our favor.
- Access the roots of our desires, which determine our motivation and choices in life.
- Access the power of empathy and compassion, which helps us create high-performing teams.
- Generate and maintain enthusiasm, cooperation, trust, confidence, and optimism.
- Break through our fears and transform them from paralysis into momentum.
- Encourage flexibility and acceptance of diversity.
- Manage stress and increase well-being.

- Read the emotions of others to anticipate appropriate actions.
- Detect resonance and dissonance with team and customers.
- Develop our intuition, create peace in our life, and generate happiness and fulfillment.
- Use and align the positive emotion with our intentions and goals to create a desired outcome.

The purpose of this section is to understand and manage your emotions in a way that will enable you to release negative ones and utilize positive ones for the optimal realization of success. Remember, your mindset—the beliefs, thoughts, and perceptions you hold about yourself, others, and the world—directs your emotions, and your emotions, in turn, affect your mindset.

I refer to all the emotions we hold in our body as our "emotion-set"—all our feelings, sensations, reactivity, intuition, emotional states, knowledge, power, sensing, reading, resonance, energy, patterns, cycles, intelligence, awareness, management, and alignment. Your emotion-set is the seat of your passion, motivation, enthusiasm, happiness, drive, and fulfillment; it is also the seat of your fears, anxiety, anger, rancor, jealousy, envy, depression, and disappointments.

In other words, your emotion-set hosts *all* feelings—positive and negative.

It doesn't really matter how optimistic we are or how determined we are to accomplish a goal. If the emotions behind our outlook and drive are negative or conflicting, we will have a hard time putting those thoughts into action and creating the life we envision.

Our emotions could very well sabotage our plans and cause the opposite of what we desire to happen. Therefore, understanding our emotions—and developing tools to direct and manage them—holds the key to our success, fulfillment, and joy in our life.

If we align our mindset by managing our minds—as we learned in Chapter 5—then we must similarly align our emotion-set by managing the emotions we hold deeply in our body.

No matter who we are or where we are in our career, we all have been conditioned by our past experiences, cultural upbringing, beliefs, myths, and traditions. Most of all, though, we all have been conditioned to disregard our emotional self.

The path to conscious leadership is strewn with the triggers of the past as we walk in the present toward the future. We're not trying to avoid our triggers or shun the messages from our body; instead, we commit to investigating these signals, looking at the emotions that surface, and working to consciously transform them. The work we do internally will change the flow of who we are as leaders and how we express ourselves in the world.

All the information that we learn about ourselves can consciously or subconsciously be unlearned, altered, or completely transformed. We realize that some of our habitual thinking patterns could cause some intense emotional patterns of fear, anger, shame, and guilt, which could become addictive and overwhelmingly intense for some. These patterns could perpetuate worry, instill doubt, and cause some to obsess over perfection.

For others, these same patterns make them fall prey to becoming a victim of people and circumstances. If we let ourselves be led by these toxic emotions that come from past experiences of failure, it becomes increasingly more difficult to become an extraordinary leader in the future, because these feelings and thoughts will consistently project imminent self-doubt and failure.

To the extent that we become conscious participants in this process of self-discovery, we can more effectively direct the changes. In other words, our success in changing any interfering thoughts, emotions, and behaviors will depend on how consciously aware we become of them.

It may be time to change what you're feeling in the moment and direct the emotion-set towards a future success and start practicing compassionate leadership.

In the following section of this final Step, I will develop, respectively, how to produce and put into practice your Leadership Emotional Logo, a visual corollary to your personal mission statement, and how to ensure your mindset is in line with your emotion-set.

STEP 4 QUICK ASSESSMENT: HOW WELL DO YOU PROGRAM YOUR EMOTIONS?

You can rate yourself, true or false from 1–10 on each question. 1 = most false, 10 = most true.

1. It's hard for me to calm down when I'm stressed.
2. I lose my temper easily when I'm frustrated or overwhelmed.
3. I react emotionally when someone disagrees with me.
4. My moods change frequently. People often call me moody.
5. I find it hard to read other people's emotions and am often surprised about their reactions.
6. I often feel physically tired, lacking energy, or depressed.
7. I find it hard to forgive and let go of negative feelings when people let me down.
8. When I'm hurt, I shut down or lash out.
9. I feel like I've lost the joy and excitement I had for my own business/ job or my life.
10. I don't know how to differentiate my emotion from the fact.
11. I give more advice to others than they care to listen to.
12. I don't know how to use emotions to fuel a positive life-giving outcome.
13. I suppress my negative emotions when they arise.
14. I have difficulties listening to people. In fact, people often tell me that I don't listen.
15. It's hard for me to build intimate relationships.

The maximum number is 150. If you answered between 100 and 150, your emotions do not empower your leadership and your life. You may either be too reactive or walled off. Developing emotional mastery and focusing on positive emotions may benefit you. You may feel happier and more fulfilled as you integrate and embody the principles of this chapter. Remember to rate yourself before and after you read this step to measure your progress.

We all know or have heard of leaders who are successful, in spite of being totally disconnected from their emotions. A few have even created value for themselves and their companies. I personally know entrepreneurs who had much success and accumulated great wealth, but as soon as they sold their business or retired, they became depressed or sick. When success is contingent upon external factors, it doesn't lead to fulfillment. When successful leaders are emotionally aware, however, they derive their happiness from within and can experience joy and fulfillment in whatever they do, independent of external success or financial wealth.

There are many *successful* leaders, of course. However, contemporary experts in social and emotional intelligence find emotional awareness and emotional management are key components to developing *great* ones.

What distinguishes a consciously aware leader from a reactive one—or even just a good one—is not their technical skills, their intelligence, or the number of followers they have. It's their ability to use their emotions to fuel and alchemize their thoughts, and change the course of their actions. It's their ability to unleash and direct the power of their emotions to make a positive difference in their life and their team. It's their capacity to control their reactivity and inspire others to do the same.

I vividly remember an incident at one of my nursing homes in Oklahoma. One day, we had a state survey. If you don't know what this means for the long-term care industry, it means terror and action. While well-intentioned, a team of auditors focus only on finding what is wrong with your organization, often without taking into consideration the commitment and the pressure the caregivers, nurses, doctors, dieticians, rehabilitation team, and support staff live under. One of my nurses, Laurie, had a big heart, but she was loud, intense, and expressed her emotions with a high-pitched voice. I had coached her many times to no avail. Her communication style was part of her personality. Unfortunately, one of the surveyors misinterpreted Laurie's tone of voice as anger, and one family member misunderstood her intentions and thought that she was arrogant. Consequently, the nursing home received a "high jeopardy deficiency," with the only remedy to let our devoted nurse go. I agonized over this decision since she was loved by many residents and by her co-workers, but had no choice but to terminate her. Laurie's dismissal affected the morale of the whole group, caused a stir in the organization, and led to the resignation of another good nurse who was not willing to continue working under the circumstances.

What I learned from this incident is that no matter what, it's impossible and ultimately detrimental to the larger mission to tamp down emotions. There are ways to encourage people to express themselves mindfully. It is time well spent to coach them to become consciously aware of cultural perceptions and how their manners and behaviors impact others. The leader is, at times, called to make tough decisions and has to do the right thing for the business, especially when the employee has been given the chance to adjust their behavior. This incident led our team to discuss openly our emotional reactions to Laurie's dismissal. The staff were encouraged to become aware and voice their fears and apprehensions regarding the display of emotions, and were supported in doing so.

Developing emotional awareness allowed space for authentic discussions to occur, and gave permission to their associates to do the same. With time, the team became a real family, supported each other, and raised the quality and efficiencies of the nursing department.

The goal of creating emotional awareness is not to change more things or to create another strategy or a new plan. Instead, it is to harness the mindset of creativity and unique strengths of every member on your team.

When you develop your emotional awareness, you give your team permission to develop theirs. Being able to lead authentically, with emotional awareness, includes the ability to intuit and connect with the emotions of your team members as well. You can only really do that by first becoming aware of your own emotion-set, knowing how to access your feelings, and directing them toward positivity and growth as a form of emotional self-control.

Emotional awareness is a key component of emotional intelligence. Emotions, like thoughts, organize themselves in patterns that repeat themselves. Becoming aware of our emotional patterns and triggers is a critical component of emotional maturity. It is the ability to take in an emotion or thought, understand it, reason with it, and regulate the emotion within yourself, then help others do the same. Those who lash out reactively struggle with controlling their emotions and can't understand why they're acting the way they are.

We all wrestle with our reactivity. That is why it is so important when we notice our reactions, that we stop and interrogate them.

Why am I feeling this way?

Where's the buildup of the negative charge coming from?

Without taking the time to pause and reflect on what's happening below the surface, we will continue to feed the beast of reactivity, deriving a sort of in-the-moment pleasure from it.

Our pause to reflect involves two levels. The first is a level of emotional *awareness*, in which we recognize what we're feeling, where we're feeling it, and why, and how we can accurately assess our emotional state. The second is a level of emotional *self-control*, in which we learn to manage our emotions with transparency, and to adapt by using our initiative and optimism each step of the way.

We cultivate emotional awareness by identifying, recognizing, and acknowledging our emotion-set, which plays an essential role in the leadership development process. Unfortunately, the business world hasn't placed much importance on teaching people how to do that. In fact, I think too often leaders are afraid that their emotions will get the better of them, and that, once they open the emotional floodgates, they won't be able to control themselves. So, they suppress them instead.

When you push away your feelings, you become out of touch with your inner self and with others. You cut yourself off from the emotions that connect you to others. As Daniel Goleman, Richard E. Boyatzis, and Annie McKee explain, great leaders depend on their emotions: "Great leaders move us. They ignite our passion and inspire the best in us. When we try to explain why they are so effective, we speak of strategy, vision, or powerful ideas. But the reality is much more primal: Great leadership works through emotions."[7]

Emotions may be hard to measure, but they can absolutely have an impact on the success of an enterprise. Increased optimism, for example, may cause a business to inaccurately assess the

---

7   Goleman, Boyatzis, and McKee, *Primal Leadership*, p. 3.

risk of a situation at hand, while increased pessimism could prevent a business from growing. Prolonged depressive moods or anxiety can negatively impact output and decrease both team cohesiveness and work satisfaction.

Notice how your mood is affected by the people sitting next to you in a meeting—sometimes by the participants' mood in general—and how people who enjoy each other's company laugh easily together.

We have all experienced this in one way or another. A person walks into the room and affects the emotion of everyone with their joyfulness and good mood. The reverse can also happen. Considering that we spend most of our time at work and that our positive outlook affects success, we should pay attention to what we want to spread: happiness or sadness?

Have you ever asked an employee how they felt about a decision that was made on a project, and they replied "Great!"? And yet, when you looked at them, they were frowning as they were uttering their answer? The problem is that it's almost impossible for people to hide their emotions. Their facial muscles, gestures, and body positions tell the real story.

While some people are good at faking it, covering up conflict can nonetheless create an emotional dissonance within themselves, which in the long run, will result in stress, burnout, a sense of not belonging, and a lack of commitment to a job. As we learned in the previous chapter, repressing the true emotion about the situation could result in a deep unease that is neither healthy for the individual nor the organization long-term.

The question is, how much should people reveal their true emotions at work? The answer lies in the culture and values of the individual and the organization. These values vary across countries, within the same country, and across industries, but—in the workplace and in public settings—employees are generally expected to subdue their emotional expression. This is a fact that has short- and long-term ramifications for individual employees, their managers, and the work culture at large.

So, what does this mean practically for a leader? It means to recognize where those feelings are coming from. Chances are, they've been activated from a past experience. Take a moment to pause and take notice of the signals you're getting from the past, the reactions you're experiencing right now.

If you want to free yourself from the recurring emotional reactions that keep driving your leadership decisions, you have to disentangle your current thoughts, behaviors, and actions from the fears and failures of your past. If you can allow the past to surface without any judgment or limitation, and cultivate the habit of questioning the real reason behind your current reactivity, you can transform your actions and their impact.

Leaders who are emotionally aware are attuned to their emotional triggers, and consciously aware of how these affect their behavior and impact others. They can use these triggers as a compass to guide and navigate their actions and to transform their unconscious reactions into conscious responses. They are more centered, more capable of flexibility, and, with a little compassion, create a sustainable environment for learning, and developing high-performing teams.

Being able to pinpoint the origin of our reactions and determine whether or not they are based on present facts or coming from a certain feeling associated with past negative experiences is a valuable emotional skill. We can become aligned with what our body (or our "gut") is telling us. We can distinguish if this is a true intuition, or a simple fear that is being triggered.

In consciously aware leadership, any resistance is an important key to bringing positive change. Why would you want to change? It is because there is an aspect of your leadership and or your life that you want to improve.

YOUR LEADERSHIP EMOTIONAL LOGO

Distinguishing the previous failures that marked your career is an essential step in the process of emotional awareness and consciously aware management. You may have forgotten some of the events that occurred, but they still impact your career, and still play a significant role in how you lead and manage your team. It is like an instrument playing in low volume in the background of your brain. No matter what you do, the instrument plays; you can't shut it off. When you try to sleep, it is there. When you wake up, it is still there. When you communicate with people, it is playing. You get so accustomed to it that you are not even aware of its sound.

In my leadership workshops, those who resisted this step, once they got it, ended up having the most sudden insights (aha moments) and reaped its greatest benefit. It is challenging to recall an incident you wanted to forget buried deeply in the past, but the prize awaiting you far exceeds your temporary discomfort. Your breakthrough is worth it! Resistance is your signal that there is something pushing you to reconsider your position.

To help you uncover and convert your negative emotions, I created a tool that I call the Leadership Emotional Logo (LEL). Each of us has a unique LEL—a pattern of emotions and reactions that are like a personal trademark—created out of personal and professional experiences of failures that are hard to forget. Think of your LEL as a visual corollary to your personal mission statement. Your LEL contains the default emotion you go to when times get tough or uncertain. Once you construct yours, you can use it to reset your reactivity at any time. It is like having a master key in your pocket. Anytime you face a closed door, you use your master key to open it.

The Leadership Emotional Logo (LEL)
The five key elements of the Leadership Emotional Logo:

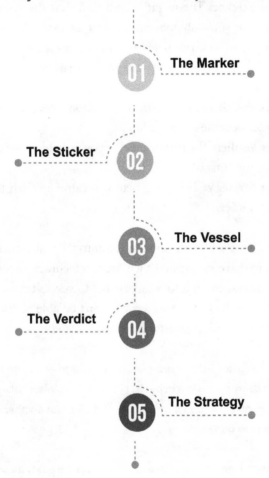

Would you like to construct yours?

First, identify the five key elements of your LEL (there is an exercise ahead to help with this):

1. **Your Marker:** A painful incident or failure that happened early on in your career and affected your professional behavior.

2. **Your Sticker:** The negative emotion that the failure generated in you—shame, guilt, regret, etc. It is like a sticker clinging to you. This negative emotion reappears every time something similar in nature to the marker occurs in the workplace.

3. **Your Vessel:** The body part or sensation where the emotion resides because of the failure.

4. **Your Verdict:** The negative belief you've held about yourself since the time of your marker.

5. **Your Strategy:** The game plan you came up with to mask your verdict.

Some failures—like the one I'm about to tell you—are so painful that we have suppressed them from our consciousness, even if we were old enough to recall them. However, if these events are not brought to the surface, we won't be able to transform our path forward in a sustainable way.

When I was twenty-three years old and about to graduate from my master's degree program in public health, my professor asked me if I could lecture on her behalf to a group of students at another campus. I was honored and excited.

Once I got to the campus, however, I discovered the lecture was in an auditorium of two hundred people, maybe more. I had prepared a presentation for thirty students, not two hundred! The crowd was loud, and several obnoxious kids were acting childish and condescendingly. I ignored them as long as I could, but I finally asked them to be quiet. It did not go well. I asked them to leave; they refused. I felt embarrassed. The whole confrontation caused me to get flustered, and I rushed through my presentation and did not perform well at the event I had been looking forward to. At twenty-three, this was a huge failure for me.

Soon thereafter, I began to be afraid of presenting in front of large crowds. To avoid similar situations, I shied away from speaking opportunities. A few years later, walking the streets of Paris where I now lived, I came across a prestigious program for public speaking. I somehow summoned the courage to sign up.

At the end of each session, the teacher would assign us a topic we had to present to the rest of the class, improvising on the spot. A winner was chosen every time, winning a symbolic pen. I finished the course with all the pens except one. My instructor could not understand why I was enrolled in the class and asked me many times why I was there. Though I had other reasons for taking the class—career advancement, refining my skill set—participating in the class helped me realize that I was capable and good enough to speak in public. Successfully presenting every week in a friendly and supportive environment helped me overcome my fear of public speaking. It also helped me identify my Marker event, which triggered my Sticker, my Vessel, my Verdict, and my Strategy.

Think of it in this way.

A **Marker** is a failure event that has marked us—marked our leadership style; it can be a failure early in our journey or perhaps a more-recent event. Identifying our marker allows us to recognize the emotional trigger that has fixed our marker in place, even when we vowed to forget it and tried not to think about it. Though we buried the emotion as deep as we could in order to move forward, it stubbornly insisted on sticking around, which influences how we reach and make decisions in the present—whether we are aware of it or not—and continues to threaten our career, our income, and our future.

Attached to the Marker are specific emotions—fear, disappointment, betrayal, mistrust, anger, or embarrassment. I call this emotion-set a **Sticker** because it sticks to you and makes itself known every time an event similar in nature to your Marker occurs.

The body responds to your Sticker by going into the fight, flight, or freeze response. That often translates into physical ailments, such as body aches or physical sensations like headache, nausea, shortness of breath, or increased heart rate. The part of your body where you experience these effects is called the **Vessel**. My vessel is my head. When I recall my Marker and experience my Sticker, I get really bad headaches.

Together, the Marker, Sticker, and Vessel work to determine the Verdict—the negative opinion you've held about yourself ever since.

To mask this Verdict, you devise a Strategy.

When I discovered that Marker event—filling in for my teacher—and deciphered my Sticker, or the painful emotions of failure and humiliation attached to the Marker, I was finally able to transform that experience from an embarrassing public failure into a joyful experience of being with an audience and delivering my best to them. Because I was no longer carrying around that negative emotion, I could remove my Sticker and clear my Vessel of unwanted, painful sensations. And, finally, I was able to overturn my previous Verdict of myself as a failure.

In business, whether we are an emerging leader or an accomplished one, we are on a journey of self-discovery through the experiences we accumulate. Many of these experiences are positive, but some of them can also be painful. I have discovered that the painful ones not only remain alive in our memories, but also influence our emotion-set and mindset in the present. Left unresolved, they will likely influence them in the future, hindering our growth as consciously aware leaders. These negative emotions are so ingrained in our psyche that they compromise any possibility of creating new, positive experiences. At times, they can prevent us from going beyond the daily work challenges into something more aligned with our core values. Why is this important? Emotions can be useful monitors of external conditions and barometers for our internal state, but they do not have to define or control us.

Once we discover our LEL, we can transcend the negative feeling that it triggers without giving it authority over us. This way our experience will stop determining our future, and we will be able to use it as an empowering tool. Whenever we recognize an emerging negative emotion, we can name it, question it, and become consciously aware of its effect in a rational way.

With continuous practice, we will be able to transform our decision-making process that is based on reaction and create conscious responses devoid of the fear or the fight, flight, or freeze response. In other words, your past leadership experiences will no longer control your present or future ones.

If we simply pay attention to how we are feeling about a decision or a project, then we can stop and ask ourselves if this feeling is incompatible with the project at hand. If it is, we can pause, recall the situation, acknowledge the fear from the past, and still move forward with our decision to take on the project. By examining and challenging our emotions, we can stop coming up with excuses or repeating the same mistakes, the same cycle of repetitive behavior that ends up producing the same outcome. It takes courage to face an incident from the past we like to forget, silence an emotion that is coming from the past, and create a visual of an experience that is coming from the future.

I believe that the LEL exercise will help you identify your default emotional pattern so that you become aware of it and reassess your decision-making process.

By completing this exercise, you'll discover the emotions that lie at the root of how you lead, and start to decipher how your emotion-set impacts your mindset. To construct your LEL, you'll have to visit this uncomfortable place, extract the emotion, and open it up for conversion from a limiting place to one that embraces development and growth.

EXERCISE: CONSTRUCT YOUR LEL.

Step 1.

Sit quietly and move into a state of relaxation by taking a few deep breaths.

Step 2.

Take a moment and think of a failure you had to face in your past. If nothing comes to mind, stop and look at some areas in your professional life where you keep getting the same results or meeting an internal resistance. Something that keeps showing up in your career that frustrates you. Write down the first situation that comes to mind.

Next, write the answers to the following questions:

1. *What is the most challenging failure you have faced in your entire career?*
2. *Describe the area in your leadership where you keep getting the same undesirable results?*

Step 3.

You may find that many failures rush into your memory. Allow them to surface. Then focus on the most frustrating one. If you remember more than one event, write down each of them. Focus particularly on the most significant one and on the earliest one. They may be the same, but if not, write them both. It's not unusual to have more than two.

You may write down as many failure events as you want. There are no right or wrong ways to answer this question. The beauty of this work is that you are just doing it for yourself. No one is watching you. No one is judging you. Just be sure not to judge yourself and stay in the flow. Wherever you land is the right place for you to be right now. Once your process is launched, it will take you deeper, and you will uncover more layers of your past. So don't worry if you feel you did not find your Marker, or if you found more than one. If you have several Marker events, they may be related through a similar theme, which you can use to sum them up. For example, I refer to my Marker as "Failure to deliver my teacher's presentation in lieu of her."

Look at the situation closely, describe it, and continue asking yourself these questions:

3. *What happened?*
4. *How did you feel about it back then? (Feel the feeling, sense the sensation, and look at that picture from the past.)*
5. *How do you feel about it now?*

Stay with the event for a bit longer. Write down as many details as you can recall. Focus on the sensory experiences: what did you see, hear, taste, touch, or smell? *Feel* the feelings that arise instead of trying to remember them. Find a way of simply being with them and noticing them. Don't be alarmed if all this remembering makes you feel upset, frustrated, or emotional. Let it be, don't judge it; simply acknowledge and name the emotions. Be sure to write these down.

Step 4.

Once you've written the long, detailed version, list your Marker(s), Sticker (s), and Vessel chronologically:

My Marker: Failing my first leadership assignment at age twenty-three to deliver my teacher's presentation in lieu of her.

Note: the same painful emotion occurred during my second leadership assignment as an assistant director of the hospital at age twenty-three, where I used power instead of collaboration to get the job done.

My sticker: Fear of failure/humiliation.

My vessel: Headache when faced with the possibility of failing.

My verdict: I am not capable enough.

My strategy: I will avoid public speaking.

Congratulations on completing this exercise. It may have been challenging. Just know that this construct for your LEL is going to help you act or not react if you decide to use this tool to transform the emotion and convert it into an energy of manifestation and creation. I use my LEL all the time. It is the number one tool I resort to whenever I react or am triggered. It helps me to quickly process my emotional state, and revert to responding instead of reacting.

We have been conditioned by our past experiences, cultural upbringing, beliefs, myths, and traditions, but most of all we have been conditioned to disregard our emotional self. This means that our false self takes leadership of our life instead of our most conscious self. The path to conscious leadership is strewn with the triggers of the past as we walk in the present toward the future. We're not trying to avoid our triggers or shun the messages from our body; instead, we commit to investigating these signals, looking at the emotions that surface, and working to consciously transform them. The work we do internally will change the flow of who we are as leaders, and how we express ourselves in the world.

THE INTERCONNECTION OF EMOTIONS AND COGNITION

To the extent that we become conscious participants in this process of self-discovery, we can more effectively direct personal and professional changes at the emotional and cognitive levels. Your emotion-set is intertwined with your Mindset and vice versa. In other words, our success in changing any interfering thoughts affects our emotions, and processing these emotions will affect our mindset and behavior. We can change the cycle of reactivity and use emotions to create a positive energy and a momentum to leap.

All the information that we learn about ourselves can consciously or subconsciously be unlearned, altered, or completely transformed. We realize that some of our habitual thinking patterns could cause some intense emotional patterns of fear, anger, shame, and guilt, which could become addictive and overwhelmingly intense for some. These patterns could perpetuate worry, instill doubt, and cause some to obsess over perfection. For others, these patterns make them fall prey to becoming a victim of people and circumstances. If we let ourselves be led by these toxic emotions that come from past experiences of failure, it becomes increasingly difficult to become extraordinary leaders in the future.

Our emotion-set is inextricably entwined with our mindset. I call them the inseparable twins. They can impact each other either in a positive or negative way. A negative belief is always associated with a negative emotion. For instance, the thought "I will never be able to convince my boss to fund this project" is connected with "I'm fearful that they'll see I'm not capable." A positive belief is always associated with a positive emotion: "I know this project is going to fly!" comes from "I haven't been this excited about anything in a long time! I got this!" Both arise from our experience.

Early on in our lives, when we start expressing our emotions, we essentially learn how to rationalize them with our thoughts.

Conversely, when we suppress them, we try not to think about them, and separate them from our thoughts.

As much as your thoughts and emotions *want* to be together, sometimes they are at odds. Like all twin siblings, they need to be separated, or given a time-out. Regardless of whether we show our emotions, or hide them away, they forever remain associated with our thoughts and beliefs.

Your mindset—what you think and what you believe—controls your emotions, and your emotions trigger your mindset.

Every thought you have produces a corresponding physical and emotional reaction. Good thoughts bring positive emotions, and bad thoughts generate negative emotions. Your thoughts create emotions. If I think that my boss overreacts, every time they call me for a one-on-one, for instance, I automatically think I'm going to be fired. My stomach churns with fear and anxiety, and I want to run away.

According to Dr. Richard Davidson, a neuroscientist, researcher, and founder of the Center for Healthy Minds at the University of Wisconsin, the brain's emotional circuits are connected to its thinking circuits. As a result, any activity in certain cognitive regions sends signals to its emotional regions. In other words, thoughts affect emotions, which affect physiology.

The interconnection of cognition and emotions has long been validated by neuroscientific research, including the work of Dr. Mary Helen Immordino-Yang and Dr. Antonio Damasio, both from USC. Their research, in which they set out to prove that "we feel, therefore we learn," involved patients who had sustained damage to their ventromedial prefrontal cortex—the part of the brain that influences the processing and expression of emotion and memory recall. As a result of the damage to this part of their cortex, the patients' social-emotional functioning was impaired. They lost the ability to perform optimally and make good decisions at work and in their relationships.

Interestingly, none of these patients had experienced previous problems in their logical reasoning, nor did they subsequently experience any lowering in their IQ. The disturbances in their brain primarily affected their emotional reactions to social contact—such as being able to demonstrate compassion, embarrassment, or guilt. They also diminished the patients' capability to evoke emotions associated with past situations, which made it impossible to respond to similar situations in the present. Though their logic and knowledge weren't compromised, they could no longer recall past emotional responses that could have guided their current reasoning process. Furthermore, they weren't able to learn from the emotional repercussions of their decisions or read the emotional reactions of their social partners.[8]

This study could not make it any clearer that emotions are an essential part of our ability to process events and make personal or business decisions. In other words, we cannot function without our emotions, even when our logic and reasoning—our mindset—are intact. Recognizing this will help us master both our mindset and our emotion-set. You can then create empowering thoughts and beliefs and start to associate positive emotions with them at will, one of the most important skills we can learn to transform our life and our leadership.

---

8   Mary Helen Immordino-Yang, *Emotions, Learning, and the Brain: Exploring the Education Implications of Affective Neuroscience* (New York: W.W. Norton & Company, 2015).

In the Align Your Mindset chapter, we learned how to catch our negative thoughts and beliefs, pause and acknowledge them, then question how they have gotten in the way of us responding objectively to our environment and circumstances. And, in the previous LEL section, we learned how to uncover the negative emotions we default to when times get tough or uncertain, which helps us control our reactivity. Now, we will learn how to *direct* our emotions as a way to determine our mindset and amplify our new beliefs. While the task is not as simple as plugging in the converter's switch, it can become a doable practice.

PROGRAM YOUR EMOTIONS AND ACCELERATE YOUR SUCCESS

The word *emotion* stems from the Latin *emovere*, which means, move out, remove, or agitate. Emotions do indeed agitate our reactions and our beliefs about ourselves and the situations we often find ourselves in.

If you can't manage your emotions, they can take on a life of their own, in a way that adversely impacts your ability to lead others. Let's say, for instance, you have an experience with a colleague or team member that makes you feel envious. You can feel it in your body—your throat might tighten, your heart beats faster, or your stomach churns with nausea. As the emotion begins to take over your thoughts, your body and mind collaborate to create a vicious cycle of physical sensations followed by you saying and doing things that you regret almost immediately. Sadly, it's not uncommon for jealousy to ruin previously close relationships with colleagues or friends.

Your emotions are the force behind your thoughts and actions.

At times, they can be quite stubborn, they seem to take on a life of their own, causing you to engage in erratic behavior you can't explain. Emotions are charged by our subconscious mind and, as such, have the power to bond with our conscious thoughts. This affects our belief systems, decision-making processes, and short- and long-term patterns of behavior.

In a very real sense, emotions create our experience of our present.

Direct your emotion set

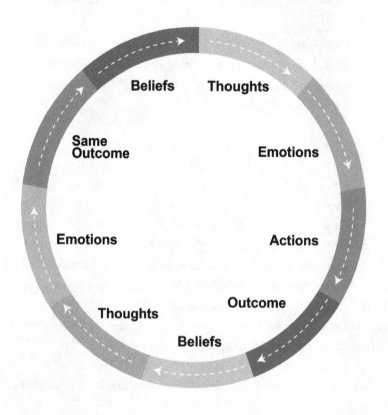

Imagine being in charge of the operations of a hospital, where eighty critically injured people are rushed to the emergency room all at once. That's what happened to me one Sunday when I was twenty-four.

In the middle of a civil war, multiple casualties arriving at our door was a familiar scene in Beirut, but the extent of this particular blast was devastating. There was no way we could accommodate all the injured—we just didn't have the capacity and I knew it. I rushed to my office to drop off my purse before heading to the ER. As I was leaving my office, a man appeared, seemingly out of nowhere, pressed a gun against my head, and forced me to sit down. He was a large, intimidating militia fighter. His face was caked with blood, and his eyes were filled with hostility and pain. He threatened to kill me if his brother did not survive his surgery in our operating room. I had no idea how this man passed security, but considering the chaos that followed the blast, I wasn't surprised. My options were limited. All that I had was my brain to assist me. I could not fight or flee, and freezing clearly wouldn't help.

Unexpectedly, a feeling of calmness came over me. I have no idea how. We started talking, and I gave the man empathy and compassion, telling him how sorry I was about his brother. I felt his pain, his anger, his fear. He then asked me to call the operating room and demanded that he attend the surgery.

I was still alive, but I knew I was running out of time. Praying for his brother to survive so I didn't end up accompanying him to heaven, I tried to tell the man about our competent staff and infection control procedures. It was as if I was talking in a vacuum. He became agitated again. I knew then that negotiating with this man was negotiating the survival of his brother. I paused and told him that if he killed me, he would also kill the possibility that his brother would survive, because I would not be able to help him or any other injured members of his group. That got his attention.

My ability to convince a violent man, who held a gun to my head, that killing me would not help his brother survive was a result of harnessing my emotions rather than letting myself be paralyzed by them. The same force of fear, when directed properly, created a power for protection and compassion.

At the same time, the fear of losing his brother made the militia man react and almost kill me, even though I had nothing to do with the incident. His fear of losing his brother was so strong, so overwhelming, that it blinded him to the reality that I was in the best position to save his brother.

Unleashing the power of emotions without processing them or knowing how to manage and direct them is a dangerous proposition. How many times have you lost control of your reactions at work—or witnessed someone else do that? How often have you blown up at a colleague in the heat of the moment, only to realize that your behavior was uncalled for? How many times have you acted on a tangle of knotty negative emotions, without first trying to untangle their meaning, and had to pay a hefty consequence for it?

To program your emotions, you first have to learn how to accurately identify them as they arise, acknowledge them and start to recognize them as opportunities for greater self-awareness and self-control. This allows you to become resilient while facing the challenges that you may face during your purpose-driven execution and to continue aligning your mindset and emotion-set to leap beyond success.

Before we proceed, I need to make a distinction between *emotions, feelings,* and *sensations.* We are accustomed to using these terms interchangeably, while in truth, they all have different meanings, all of which can help us to see our experiences more clearly. Here are some simple distinctions that will help clarify how I am using these terms. Let's start with *emotions* and *feelings.*

Emotions are physiological experiences that are triggered by internal or external events. Emotions are somatic, meaning, literally, "of the body." We may not be conscious of emotions, while they are arising, but they can be objectively measured by physical factors like blood flow, brain activity, and facial expressions. When we are afraid of something, for example, our hearts begin to race, our mouths become dry, our skin turns pale, and our muscles contract. This emotional reaction occurs automatically and unconsciously.

Feelings, meanwhile, are secondary. They live in our minds, where they register our subjective experience of emotions once they have occurred. Feelings give meaning to our emotions and physiological response to them through the language we use to describe them. Think of it this way: feelings are our impressions and interpretations of our emotions.

People sometimes have difficulty connecting their feelings to their emotions because they're not fully aware of their emotions. They may express feelings of anger, for instance, but they are experiencing an emotion of fear. Only when we can name our emotions can we start to describe where in the body we feel this emotion and start to become more emotionally aware.

Sensations are the physiological component of an emotional

experience. They help us recognize the emotional experience because they are physical. We may feel pain, discomfort, a tingling sensation, or tension as the body reacts to being triggered emotionally. These sensations are important to detect so that you can preempt your emotional reactions and take time to process them before you react.

Emotional awareness means being able to identify and manage one's own emotions, feelings, and sensations—as they come up. It is a state of emotional wakefulness. It is understanding the nature of the emotional prompts buried in our subconscious, a process of purposefully observing and naming the feelings as they arise, being able to decipher the negative ones and transform them into appropriate responses during situations high in emotions. It is bringing awareness to our negative beliefs and thoughts and encoding them with positive emotions.

When people are emotionally awake, they have access to peace and fulfillment, regardless of their circumstances. They derive their happiness from within. Since the source of their happiness lies within, they can create whatever they want without being threatened. Their sense of survival is not dependent upon their success.

What about you? Are you looking for something different, more, or better in your life? Could your emotions direct your way?

Emotions give us easy access to the subconscious mind. If we trace a powerful emotion that conflicts with our ideas or statements back in time, we will no doubt find it intertwined with our past conditioning. While this may seem like a relatively innocent journey into the mind, it can stir up some deeply buried emotions. If that happens, slow down, or back off, before you try again. It's important work, because the more we suppress these past emotions, the more they show up in our present reactions. If we want to reprogram our mindset with a new belief, but the emotion associated with this belief is not congruous with it, we often repeat our past narratives, which is not what we're going for.

Here's an example of how emotions can sabotage thinking. Let's say you have been promoted to director of a special project, just as Joe—in the previous section—was charged with a high-profile project. Everyone believes you are the one to lead it. You are scared, however. The last time you were put in charge was a disaster. As a result, you now spend the bulk of your time second-guessing yourself, avoiding risks at all costs. Your fear has created a visceral, emotional response that keeps you from being present and effective. Remember, emotions are powerful. They are the energetic link to the brain and, as such, determine our actions. Without encoding a new emotion-set, any attempt to transform our negative beliefs, experiences, and actions will be in vain.

According to the neuroscience expert Christine Comaford, author of *The New York Times* bestseller *Smart Tribes: How Teams Become Brilliant Together*, our emotional brain drives 90 percent of our behaviors, while our intellect controls only 10 percent of our decision-making.

Emotions support and guide our higher-level cognitive processes. Only when we recognize this essential role will we be able to lead and contribute in a meaningful way, directing our emotions to drive the positive change in our lives. Without such direction, our emotions could easily manifest the opposite of our intended outcome. To effect that change, you must harness the power of your emotions. By attaching an intense emotion like desire or passion to the belief, you create whatever you long for in your life and in your business.

Direct your emotion set

Should you want to create a limitless "you" and accelerate success, it may be time to learn about "emotional mastery." Wiring your emotions to your new belief matrix will help you do that and escape, once and for all, from your own "dream trap." This trap keeps you from pursuing your dreams and going beyond success.

Unfortunately, negative experiences are inevitable. They occur daily. Because each one is inextricably linked to a strong negative emotion, the effects of those experiences (no matter how long ago they happened) can linger in the nervous system for a long time. While some of us can shake off undesirable, negative emotions quickly, others have difficulties doing so. When you feel let down, judged, embarrassed or angry, it can easily affect your work and your relationships until you release the emotion.

To program your emotions is to learn how to extract them from your experiences, release the negative ones and replace them with the positive ones. We can all remember the emotions of joy generated by gratifying events in our life such as success, graduation, marriage, birth of a child. Drawing out the positive emotions from pleasurable experiences and using them to generate positive beliefs about yourself will help you accelerate your success. The same way you associate the positive emotions with an image or a goal you want to manifest, you can associate the positive emotions and feelings to create positive affirmations about yourself.

Thoughts affect our emotions and vice versa which will generate our actions and create an outcome that can bring about new beliefs. This, in turn, will generate new thoughts and create new emotions, causing a new outcome. Mastering the process of programming new emotions will support you in aligning your mindset and your emotion-set with your purpose and creating success by design.

EXERCISE: PROGRAM YOUR EMOTIONS.

In this exercise, you will learn how to release the negative emotions from an unpleasant experience and use the positive ones to empower your success.

Step 1.

Sit quietly and move into a state of relaxation by taking a few deep breaths.

Step 2.

Bring to the surface an unpleasant experience. It could be a big deal. *(My business partner just announced they're leaving the company, I'm on my own, and I'm scared.)* or something less significant. *(My boss yelled at me for forgetting a meeting I was supposed to attend, and now I am so ashamed and embarrassed).* Take a few moments to relive the scene and then write it down in as much detail as you can, recalling your feelings, and how they manifested in your body.

Step 3.

Extract the learnings from your experience.

Step 4.

Be grateful and appreciate the lesson.

Example: *I am so grateful for who I became as a result of this learning, or I appreciate learning that this method or strategy does not work.*

Remember there is always something to be learned in any situation.

Step 5.

Think of a success story or a big achievement you accomplished in your past. Visualize it and bring it closer to your memory.

Example: *I remember the awards ceremony when I was honored for creating a successful program for Alzheimer's care. I was so happy and felt so proud that we were able to positively affect the lives of so many of our patients.*

Step 6.

Just like you did in Step 2, take a moment to feel into that experience. Write about it in as much detail as you can. What was the predominant sensation in your body? Can you bring that forward and extract the emotion from it?

Step 7.

Now, build a new affirmation by attaching the positive emotion to it that you've just extracted from your experience. Go back to the disempowering experience you wrote about, and replace the negative emotions with the new, empowering one that emphasizes the learning. Choose a different narrative.

Example: *I am unstoppable, I am successful at creating my own business without relying on a partner,* or *I don't take things personally, and I look for the gold in any situation.*

Don't get discouraged if you can't find the gold right away. Sometimes it shows up after the experience. While you're going through something you don't always realize you've become stronger and more empowered.

Step 8.

Visualize, feel, affirm, and repeat your new affirmation until it replaces the negative one. In doing this, you are empowering your mind by associating the positive emotion with the experience and offering up a new blueprint—one that focuses on the learning in each situation and the positive feelings that emerge. The more you repeat and reiterate your success and feel it at a deeper level, the more you encourage success.

Of course, positive experiences are associated with positive emotions and they, too, can remain in the body for a long time, *positively* affecting your work and your life. You want to hold on to those.

KEY TAKEAWAYS TO PROGRAM YOUR EMOTIONS

- Leaders who are emotionally aware are attuned to their emotional triggers. They can use these triggers as a compass to guide and navigate their actions and to transform their unconscious reactions into conscious responses.
- Leadership Emotional Logo: LEL. An important tool to be able to process and direct emotions is the leadership emotional logo: The Marker—The Sticker—The Vessel—The Verdict—The Strategy.
- Accelerate success and affect the cycle of change as you learn how to program your emotions: Release the negative ones and use the positive ones to empower yourself and generate positive outcomes.

CHAPTER 5

LEAP

"Do not follow where the path may lead. Go instead where there is no path and leave a trail."

—RALPH WALDO EMERSON

Once you discover how to **Lean** into your passion and **Execute** from your purpose, you are no longer acting without a plan. Instead, you are making the commitment to lead a purpose-driven life. By executing from your vision and purpose, you start to work for—and from—your emerging future. When you bring conscious awareness to your thoughts, beliefs, emotions, and actions, you begin to support balance and harmony in your life and the lives of others around you, because you are able to **Align** your mindset and **Program** your emotions in service to your purpose. You now have the tools to create limitless success and fulfillment in your life and in your business. The caveat of becoming extremely successful is that at times the ego takes over and some leaders become arrogant, obsessed with their power, and think that they are invincible. Can't we all name some egocentric and megalomaniac leaders? When leaders realize that leadership is no longer about them, but the effect of their leadership on others, they choose to use the momentum of success to elevate others around them. This is when they are ready to leap beyond success.

In this book's final chapter, you will learn how to integrate the transformative experience of the L.E.A.P. steps into a wider vision—from the individual to the collective, and from the boardroom to the world at large. Applying these four steps in your everyday life will enable you to leap without fear of criticism or failure, with total confidence in your vision and your abilities, and in total harmony with the external systems around you.

STEP 5 QUICK ASSESSMENT: EVALUATE YOUR READINESS TO LEAP

Rate yourself from 1–10 on each question. 1 = mostly false, 10 = mostly true.

1. My list of priorities is focused on how I can accomplish more social impactful actions than personal acquisitions.
2. My personal mission, purpose, and goals are aligned with a greater mission and purpose to benefit others along with me.
3. I pay attention to the means of my actions, and do not believe that the means justify the ends.
4. I always lead from my passion and not out of obligation.
5. My end goal is fulfillment and contribution beyond personal success.
6. I always take responsibility for my actions even when I am incited by others to take these actions.
7. I have no problem selecting a project from the unknown future even when my past experience is different.
8. My financial success is a means to do social good around me.

9. I always execute on my goals and ask for help when I need it.

10. I recognize my emotional triggers and redirect them to fuel and manifest my vision.

11. I am willing to change my point of view and challenge my beliefs in order to evolve.

12. I use my intuition and can recognize when it is biased by past experience.

13. I let passion and compassion fuel my future actions even when they present a challenge for my beliefs.

14. I strive for personal fulfillment and understand that success without it is the ultimate failure.

15. I purposefully help people around me succeed, and understand that my success alone when people around me fail is the utmost disappointment.

The maximum score on this section is 150 points. If you are between 100 and 150, congrats. You are ready to leap! You will be able to set an example for people around you and coach them to succeed and go beyond to help others do so as well. If you are below 50 points, that's okay; please don't be hard on yourself. Maybe you've attained success but are not fulfilled.

I recommend that you set an intention for yourself to go beyond yourself. Hopefully, the tools in this chapter will help you achieve this goal.

INNOVATE, EVOLVE, AND LEAP

As business leaders, we are constantly looking for new ways to **innovate, evolve, and leap.** Additionally, as individuals, part of the natural order of things is that we are continuously evolving. Individually and collectively, we build on the progress of previous eras to innovate and grow into something new. A leap could bypass the normal progression and create an evolutionary great jump from one level to an unimagined one. This is true with scientists, mathematicians, philosophers, and theologians, all of whom have proudly stood on the shoulders of giants to advance humanity's vision of what is possible.

This is also true for leaders who have within their power the ability to decide how they continue to move forward collectively. Think of it in much the same way the Canadian geese fly in formation, working as one, serving each other to get where they're going.

Leaping occurs as a breakthrough. It is a precipitous and radical act of transformation which at first may appear foolish, absurd, or unreasonable. It changes the natural progression of things, and ultimately alters the way we think, feel, and behave. It is a sudden jump to a great height in our evolution. When people leap through breakthroughs, they need a landing space to hold them. Think about any of your own breakthroughs, how you felt about people around you, and how they reacted to your sudden transformation. Through the L.E.A.P. process, we can have many awakenings leading to the growth and development of our mindset and emotion-set. As we embody the different steps, we land on more solid grounds.

For the sake of this method, I like to define leaping as transcending our personal success. Instead, we are Foreseeing future possibilities individually and collectively as we interrupt the past, Foretelling as we enroll stakeholders, and Forereaching as we execute smartly—all while sensing the needs of the fields around us. Leaping can occur as a result of incremental progression over time, or a sudden transformational jump.

I like to think of evolving, innovating, and leaping as an informed and impassioned selection of a possible future that we're making a reality. What makes us evolve is our ability to innovate. How we think, select, and manage the possibility of our future determines the nature of our evolution. While evolving and innovating may be a slow process of progression, a well-timed leap propels us quicker to this transformative end.

Once we master the four L.E.A.P. steps, we can finally act in accordance with a shared vision of innovation and evolution. This will generate personal and professional breakthroughs that lead to a more positive net impact for every stakeholder and every member of the community. Elevating leadership beyond success requires another awakening: the big realization that the most important role leaders can have is to serve others. This deep shift occurs when leaders start leading through compassion and extending far beyond their personal gains into societal gains, influencing the future of business and humanity. I call this breakthrough becoming a **leaper**.

LEAP INTO THE TRIPLE-WIN PARADIGM

Now, it's time to lay a collective foundation for a paradigm of leadership committed to creating a positive impact on our culture. This foundation, which is anchored by the four L.E.A.P. steps, is strengthened by the twin pillars of authenticity and integrity. It empowers you to move beyond the singular self, and begin to consider your impact on others. You start prioritizing your interconnectedness with, and your responsibility towards, the systems around you that are now more closely connected to your passion and your purpose.

Business today is no longer "business as usual." Leaders must manage far more than strategic plans, competitors, and resources. They are now also expected to be inspirational, to motivate their teams, and to be a force for social good—all while turning a profit and dealing with technologically evolving times. It's little wonder that many feel overwhelmed by the task. How are they supposed to meet all these demands at once?

As we intentionally cultivated our awareness and deliberately engaged in the process of transformation, we experienced our inner power transform. In doing so, we gained more control of our behavior, reactive and proactive alike, and became the leader we were born to be.

When we become aware of how our interior condition impacts the outcome of our actions, we start shifting our undertakings to create more good around us. This shift empowers us to become inspirational.

Leaders who leap, or **leapers**, inspire through their beingness, actions, and values. They create a conscious culture in which team members feel valued and encouraged to attain their full potential. Through their own work on personal transformation, these leapers impact their families, help create thriving workplaces and communities, and prompt change in the world around them.

Leapers are triple winners. They are successful and create organizations engaged in authentic missions beyond self-interest. In the process, they co-create a future that benefits corporations, their participants, and the communities in which they live in such a way that satisfies every stakeholder in a **triple-win**

paradigm: you win / I win / the world wins. Through their contribution to the world around them, they move beyond success. In becoming a leaper, the leader's greatest win is self-fulfillment as they create their legacy.

Thankfully, over the past few decades, we have started to see a new paradigm emerging in business. In 2019, the Business Roundtable of CEOs publicly redefined the Purpose of a Corporation to Promote "An Economy That Serves All Americans."[9]

The statement was signed by 181 CEOs, all of whom committed to lead their companies for the benefits of all stakeholders, moving away from shareholders' primacy to now include a commitment to customers, employees, suppliers, and communities. Similarly, amazing leaders and entrepreneurs, funded by impactful investors, are creating purpose-driven organizations. Practiced at a large scale, this will hopefully cause leadership to leap into the triple-win paradigm.

When leaders leap, civilization leaps and we can collectively emerge into a new paradigm of leadership—we all leap!

When leaders develop an inner conscious awareness through the four L.E.A.P steps, they start creating subtle shifts in how they relate to people and systems around them. They start recognizing different systems from a perspective that includes them. They become more present to the experiences of other people and the fields around them. They move their attention from their own ego to a larger ecosystem of concern, focused

---

9 "Business Roundtable Redefines the Purpose of a Corporation to Promote 'An Economy that Serves All Americans'," Business Roundtable, August 19, 2019, https://www.businessroundtable.org/business-roundtable-redefines-the-purpose-of-a-corporation-to-promote-an-economy-that-serves-all-americans.

at once on their surrounding social, economic, and political arenas. They begin to experience the influence of their actions and decisions on their family, community, and other groups of interests.

The capacity of leaders to become triple-winners, or leapers, is correlated with their capacity to become compassionate, to embrace change, and to evolve and innovate from an emerging future independent from what was possible in the past.

HOW DOES COMPASSION HELP US LEAP?

In our L.E.A.P journey, we have rediscovered our authentic nature and learned to contribute from it. Our journey evolves from passion to compassion as we create our legacy on the way.

We often use the terms compassion, empathy, and love inter-changeably—even though they don't exactly mean the same thing. They are all positive emotions that can pull us towards each other in an altruistic way, yet they can create a different experience of leadership.

Understanding what a team member or a partner is feeling, and taking a stand to help them, is different from shouldering their pain in a way that lifts their burden but adds to yours. "Connect with empathy, but lead with compassion"—beautifully stated by Hougaard, Carter, and Afton in the *Harvard Business Review*. Based on their research and their experience, they find that compassion goes beyond empathy.

Empathy, according to Hougaard, is a close visceral understanding of the other person's experience. If we lead from empathy, at times we may take on other people's feelings, we may become biased, and our judgment may become cluttered.[10] Some leaders can't make important decisions regarding their business because of it. I am guilty of it myself. At times, I gave employees chances over chances because I empathized with their personal stories, which ended up being bad business decisions. We can all be trapped that way.

Love is the highest feeling on the spectrum of creation, creativity, life fulfillment, and happiness. The right to love and be loved is real. On the other end of the spectrum is fear. Most of our actions are either driven by love or by fear. We are either looking to increase pleasure or avoid pain.

Compassion, on the other hand, is a deep understanding of others while taking a stand for empowering and coaching them to deal with their own problems.

It is a kind emotion towards a person or a group while being present without judgment, guilt, or fear—just total acceptance and kindness. It is a feeling of connection towards the other. Although it is a genuine desire to collaborate with them, it is also a stand and a belief that they are capable of handling their challenges. The most compassionate leaders are highly collaborative. They work alongside their people to make things happen. They use inspiring words such as "we" and "together." To that end, compassion helps them develop social and interpersonal skills, connections, interactions, and better communications.

---

10   Rasmus Hougaard, Jacqueline Carter, and Marissa Afton, "Connect with Empathy, but Lead with Compassion," *Harvard Business Review*, December 23, 2021, hbr.org/2021/12/connect-with-empathy-but-lead-with-compassion.

Being compassionate helps us connect with others, and repair relationships while respecting our boundaries. It empowers others while fostering emotional intelligence and well-being.

Empathy is to feel what another person is feeling; **Love** is a feeling of deep affection; **Compassion** is empathy towards someone that includes a willingness to empower them to handle their own suffering.

Not all leaders find it easy to acknowledge a connection with those they work with. As a result, they struggle to be liked and often come across as cold, aloof, or reserved. Some leaders don't know how to empower their teams, preferring to do everything themselves rather than delegating. They tend to operate solo, especially entrepreneurs, and they struggle with group dynamics. They might think of themselves as compassionate for taking on more responsibilities and letting others off the hook. But that's not compassionate leadership! On the contrary, being compassionate means tuning into others, holding them accountable, and knowing when to push them harder and when to ease up—helping them attain success and fulfillment.

In my experience, I've found the easiest access to love, compassion, and empathy is through actively listening. Whenever I practice listening without judging someone, and listening for real possibilities, I access compassion towards another. I also access compassion towards myself when I stop judging or feeling sorry for myself, or feeling guilty about something I should or shouldn't have done.

Compassion and empathy promote contribution and service. Inspiring leaders want their people to develop. They invest in them, and they encourage activities that foster physical, intellectual, emotional, and spiritual growth and well-being. Through emotional understanding, empathy, acknowledgment, and appreciation, we all can inspire our teams and motivate them.

Competition also takes on a different flavor when you practice compassionate behavior. Instead of working against your competitors, you can adopt an attitude of working *towards* improving on their products or services, complementing them by further differentiating and supplementing your products and services through innovations. I know of a great leader who told me this: "To be successful, do things differently, and do them exceedingly well." This great leader happens to be my husband!

As I became a more compassionate individual, I became more sensitive to people around me and their needs. Some time ago, as a leader of my organization, I started dedicating time in the beginning of our meetings for staff to share personal news and professional concerns, if they wished to do so. Sharing at a personal level is a tricky proposition in a professional setting—you never know how the information is processed and used by some members. The appropriate thing to do is to establish a safe environment to share about our professional challenges. As trust grows among team members, I noticed that they started sharing how work is affecting their personal lives, health, and well-being. Together, we established a context for confidentiality. Participating members could not gossip about, hint at, or talk about anything they heard during these pre-meeting check-ins. This created a background of relatedness and understanding among team members, and helped strengthen everyone's sense of belonging and safety. It also helped them relax and put aside their personal worries at work, and focus on the business needs. It never failed. When we were able to create the context and set time for checking in at the beginning of our meetings, we were able to create cohesiveness among our leaders while increasing their level of satisfaction. As moods are contagious, they tend to permeate all stratas of the organization, creating a positive general momentum.

Once we started this practice, I noticed how compassionate they became towards each other. Their support of each other extended to the departments they were leading, our turnover improved, so did our quality care. The team took ownership of their nursing centers. The different homes started collaborating together instead of competing against each other. Their core competencies improved and got differentiated, which enabled us to innovate further in the fields of wellness and integrative medicine. We were moving towards the triple-win paradigm!

THE LOVE AND COMPASSION WE SEEK MUST BEGIN WITHIN

It is very hard to love others when we don't love ourselves. It is simply impossible to give what we don't have. I am not referring here to selfishness, entitlement, and indulgence to justify that we come first and are entitled to get things before others. Rather, I'm talking about a deeply felt sense of kindness and affection towards ourselves and our true nature.

Self-compassion is treating yourself with patience and kindness—as if you are your own best friend. In fact, studies have found that individuals who are more self-compassionate tend to be happier and more satisfied in their relationships. They seem to cope better in stressful situations and setbacks.[11] A researcher at the University of Texas at Austin named Kristin Neff found that self-compassion makes people less anxious, depressed, and

---

11   Carley Hauck, "How Leaders Build Trust at Work Through Authenticity," Mindful.org, March 17, 2021, https://www.mindful.org/how-leaders-build-trust-at-work-through-authenticity/.

self-critical. It also made people more confident, productive, supportive of others, and physically healthier.

Not surprisingly, the main blocks to self-compassion are self-criticism, feeling unworthy of love, and resenting being vulnerable or appearing weak. Negative self-talk, feelings of inadequacy, or beliefs that you are not enough are not empowering. They are demoralizing. Such self-criticism undermines self-confidence and leads to fear of failure.

Dr. Neff also found that many successful leaders are reluctant to turn their kindness inward. Most of us know how to support others, but do not treat ourselves the same way. Self-compassion is a critical component of good leadership. It's not a sign of weakness or vulnerability; quite the opposite. It is a sign of strength and clarity. As a leader, when you stand up for yourself, you teach people how to be treated. You are not passive or aggressive, but you have clear boundaries and don't allow people to overstep them or disrespect you. You encourage others, by example, to skillfully set boundaries for themselves and to respect others. You become truer to yourself without feeling guilty about it. By extension, you become more compassionate toward others, respect their boundaries, and listen openly to their views and opinions.

As a leader who practices self-compassion, you will generate and maintain enthusiasm, cooperation, trust, confidence, and optimism. Compassion toward yourself and others provides you access to contribution, service, and partnerships.

The key is to treat yourself with the same support and understanding when you fail as you would treat your friends when they are struggling. Treat yourself with kindness and don't be judgmental. When you are struggling, stop for a moment and ask yourself what you need to support yourself, both in the moment and in the future. Recognize that we are all imperfect, and we all lead imperfect lives. If for no other reason, do this because, ultimately, self-compassion makes you more motivated and resilient than self-criticism.

The foundation of self-compassion is conscious awareness, the ability to be present with what's happening as it's happening—to have the courage to be with difficult emotions and not avoid them or fight them. Forgiveness is an integral part of self-compassion. When we forgive others, we are freeing ourselves from the emotional hold the other person has on us.

In our culture, we have blocks to self-compassion, which create a vicious cycle: harsh self-criticism makes us afraid of failure, which increases our anxiety. We start failing more often, lose confidence in ourselves, and decide that self-criticism is warranted. Research has shown that the more we are able to support ourselves in the face of failure and pick ourselves up and try again, the more likely we are to succeed again. In the same way we motivate others, we can motivate ourselves. Self-compassion helps us to thrive.

A few years ago, an eighty-two-year-old veteran commander, Jim, and his wife participated in a workshop I gave in New York. When I talked about self-love and forgiveness, the wife kept nudging her husband to speak. Finally, he stood up and shared an experience he had during the Vietnam War. When he was a commander, his battalion went for a maneuver while he stayed behind. None of them came back, which made him the only survivor. Soon after the war, he partially lost his hearing and his sight, but he fully lost his desire for any kind of social life. He retreated into solitude, steeped in survivor's guilt. Something opened for him, though, during the following exercise, which helped him forgive himself and accept what happened without narrating it with his negative self-talk.

For most veterans, survival guilt is frequent. It is this feeling that they bring home with them that does not let them rest. It generates shame and self-loathing, and it triggers post-traumatic stress disorder (PTSD) and all its emotional reactions. Survivors bear a sense of responsibility around what happened and carry it with them, heavy on their shoulders. Many participants with previous trauma found retrieving their leadership emotional logo in the last step of L.E.A.P. a particularly helpful tool. In Jim's case, his vessel was his hearing and eyesight. Over the years of being triggered, he became more remorseful and lost interest in life. But with time, Jim was able to forgive himself as he was able to process his emotions and change his beliefs about himself.

I kept in touch with this couple and marveled at how Jim was able to reverse his PTSD reactions. He was able to intercept the cycle of emotions that we covered in the previous chapter. He found his passion. His wife accompanied him to gatherings where he was able to talk to groups and, at his level, he became a change maker to people who suffered from trauma. Jim turned the narrative of his story around. He discovered a purpose for his life: to help veterans with PTSD change their life. The change in him was so sudden. It took the form of a breakthrough and did not leave a dry eye when it happened during the workshop. His sudden metamorphosis is the perfect example of leaping at any age independently of one's circumstances. The deeper the fall, the higher the jump and the greater the leap. I commend my commander-in-chief Jim every day for his services to our country, and for encouraging me to pursue my passion.

EXERCISE: HOW TO PRACTICE SELF-COMPASSION

Step 1.

Sit quietly and move into a state of relaxation by taking a few deep breaths.

Step 2.

Think of something that you blame yourself for, something you're ashamed of. Write it down.

Step 3.

Validate your emotion. Feel the emotion. Consciously bring your awareness to the fact that you are suffering: *This is hard right now. I am suffering.* If you can, name the emotion you are feeling, and tell yourself that it is ok to feel this emotion.

Step 4.

Come up with examples of people going through the same situation or worse. Bring them into your mind and empathize with them.

Step 5.

Recognize the ways in which your situation is better than theirs.

Step 6.

Think of three examples of success in your own career or life; remember how you felt back then. Spend time reliving those emotions.

Step 7.

Bring words of loving-kindness to yourself. Add some gesture of kindness—maybe put your hands on your heart or on your belly. Or give yourself a hug, silently offering words of support. Feel the emotion of success you felt back then right now.

Compassion and self-kindness help us deal with fear and anxiety. They help us overcome self-loathing, remorse, and even deal with PTSD like in Jim's case.

What tools can we use that would allow us to overcome our fear and anxiety, and help empower the people around us to do the same?

One technique that has helped me throughout my life is to separate the parts of me that feel worthless or not good enough from my true self. Any time those feelings surface, I practice self-love or self-empathy. When I hear that voice or belief again that reminds me I am no good at sports—I lovingly set it aside. I acknowledge its existence because it is there, but I thank it, and gently remind it that it is not me. It is not coming from my true self but from old fears. I then tell myself that I love who I am, including all my fears.

Using the language of empathy is a powerful tool to convert fear into courage; it can carry over an array of feelings that can affect the quality of achievements and work outcomes if it is used as a conversion metric. I started befriending the thoughts of failure with a sentence that I love using: *So what?*

We are all far beyond what we achieve and far beyond what we can create, dream, or conceive.

In order to leap, we have to harness the power of compassion and to convert fear into a positive emotion.

EXERCISE: HOW TO USE COMPASSION TO TRANSFORM FEAR

Step 1.

Sit quietly and move into a state of relaxation by taking a few deep breaths.

Step 2.

Think of something that you are afraid of. Write it down.

Step 3.

Give compassion to yourself. Practicing compassion could be just giving yourself a hug and saying, "I love you even if you are afraid."

Step 4.

Go back to the "why" seven times. Why are you in this business, organization, team, or taking on this project or task? Write your "why" seven times. You may notice you have a different answer each time, and your seventh answer is nothing like the first one.

Step 5.

Find something you are grateful for and amplify the feeling of being grateful for it. Write it down.

Step 6.

Keep feeling compassion, empathy, gratitude, and commit to your unique expression of your gift.

Step 7.

Go back to your vision, goal, and task and attach the emotion of gratitude and pleasure to it. Write it down.

THE INTUITIVE MIND: A GUIDE ON OUR WAY TO LEAP

Albert Einstein famously wrote: "The intuitive mind is a sacred gift, and the rational mind is a faithful servant. We have created a society that honors the servant and has forgotten the gift." So how could we honor the sacred gift of intuition and let it guide the faithful servant of rational decision-making?

Your intuition, referred to at times as "gut feeling," represents your inner voice of wisdom. As we learn to recognize our emotions and their effects on us and others, we start developing our gut instinct. We start paying attention to it and, depending on its clarity, we start following it. I like to think of intuition as my future self whispering in my ear what to do next, and my faithful guide to sense the fields around me. I like to define the fields around me as social, economic, political, scientific, medical, technology, etc., including the more encompassing field of conscious awareness—referred to by scientists as the quantum field, and by spiritualists as the spiritual field of existence.

Executives often question information that contradicts their intuition, and rely on their hunches to make decisions.

Initially, as we started innovating in the field of integrative and complementary medicine, the state surveyors criticized some of our practices like massage therapy, art, music, and group therapies, knocking our integrative approaches to our health and nursing care. Ironically, the same state surveyor joined our team a few years later, eventually stating that our innovations were ahead of their time. Once she witnessed the impact of the quality of our care on our residents, she became our strongest advocate.

As we continued to innovate and "presence" information far beyond what we thought was possible in the fields of wellness and integrative medicine, one of our nursing homes made a leap in its geriatric psychiatric care, reducing medications to previously unheard-of levels. The results were immediate and dramatic, and so impressive a famous psychiatrist joined our organization and used our model of care to enhance his research. Within a year, the nursing home won the mention of Zero deficiency, the best care possible in nursing homes, and our network-wide success and innovation continued on an exponential curve. We won several awards in quality of care and employee satisfaction.

Touring different care facilities, I could not help but notice the level of calmness in our patients, from the Alzheimer's unit to the ones that housed some of our most agitated cognitively impaired patients, particularly when our director of nursing, Nancy, was on duty. One day, as I was touring the nursing home, I asked her about her secret. She giggled and, with her beautiful smile and kind demeanor, nonchalantly said,

"You know, I pray with the team every morning before we start our day!" Every single morning, the care plan meeting started with a prayer for the patients and staff with an invocation of higher wisdom to guide the staff's actions. The team created an intention for the day that served the highest good for every stakeholder.

I started researching prayers, meditation, and healing for the cognitively impaired and stumbled upon Norman Shealy, MD, President of Shealy-Sorin Wellness Institute and Holos Energy Medicine Education. Often called the "Father of Holistic Medicine," he founded the American Holistic Medical Association in 1978. I was able to recruit a student of his, named Ann, who regularly toured specific sites. Every time Ann visited, the team witnessed a calmness among patients that lasted almost a week at a time. Whether the staff believed in the power of prayers, energy healing, or simply calming our spirit through breathing techniques, they invariably reported a noticeable change and a marked improvement in our patient's well-being and, just as importantly, a reduced level of medications.

This discovery inspired some of us to explore further the phenomena of the invisible and the frontiers of energy medicine, which further empowered us to innovate and develop more L.E.A.P.-based pillars in our approach to wellness and integrative care. As a result, it emboldened us to start evolving from the future and leap into new levels. During each step, I personally relied on my intuition to guide my choices and help me sense the field of energy medicine.

According to a study run by The Economist Intelligence Unit (EIU) in which they surveyed 174 leading organizations, nine out of ten executives rely on their gut feeling in making business decisions. When evidence and our intuition are mismatched, we experience what is called cognitive dissonance, like the dissonance we experienced in Step 3 of Aligning our Mindset when our beliefs and intentions mismatched.[12]

The problem is, we don't always know how to interpret what our intuition is pointing out, which is why we too often confuse unconscious bias with intuition's voice of forward-thinking wisdom. So how can you distinguish between a genuine intuition and an unconscious bias?

The simple answer is your intuition guides you, and an unconscious bias blocks you. Your intuition informs your body in the moment if you pay attention to it. You just have to stop and notice if there is an expansion or a constriction in your body. Your emotions are valuable signals, directing you toward your intuition and urging you to leap with total confidence into the future you most want to realize.

If we can reflect on a decision with unbiased facts, and better understand the emotional triggers from the past, we can then differentiate these feelings with accuracy.

When the facts support a decision, and you still feel uneasy about it, you may want to examine if fear is getting in the way. As we distinguished our emotional logo in Step 4 of this book, the use of intuition in business becomes easier. If the fear comes from our emotional logo and the belief about ourselves associated with it, it means that it is coming from the past and most probably pointing us in the wrong direction. However, if the uneasy feeling does not have its roots in our fear or emo-

12   Charlie Taylor, "Executive Decision Making Often Relies on Gut Instinct," *The Irish Times*, September 26, 2014, www.irishtimes.com/business/executive-decision-making-often-relies-on-gut-instinct-1.1941621.

tional logo, then it is emerging from the future—and our future self—steering us in the right direction.

How do you know if the decision you are about to make is emerging from the future?

Take a moment to examine the emotion arising from your gut feeling.

If there is fear, you ought to assess if it is coming from the past.

If it is peaceful, then you have a green light to go for it.

Many business leaders make use of their intuition. When I started paying attention to my intuition in life and in business, my life shifted significantly. I eliminated hesitation and regret from my decision-making process. In the past, when I did not listen to my intuition, I created a lot of ambiguity for others and some conflict within.

When I look back at my life, I realize that most of the decisions that I made spontaneously as "love at first sight," without any external influence, were my happiest and most rewarding ones. On the other hand, the ones that involved lots of back and forth and hesitation went either way. Many of my business-leader friends who are greatly successful have also developed their business gut feeling.

As leaders thrive, they develop skills, processes, and strategies for their winning ventures. In other terms, they become more effective at detecting how certain projects triumph. Even though some plans have all the ingredients for a predictable success, unforeseen events may happen, which make the project flop. In my business, I passed up some opportunities that made business sense to watch some owners' developers tank the enterprise. The reverse has also happened to me and, most of the time, what was blocking me from embracing an opportunity was fear of failure.

They start making decisions from the future informed by their intuition.

Once we possess the tools to interpret our intuition with clarity and purpose, we can then rely on it to guide us.

The successful business, and the reliable leadership team that we built, helped me realize that my passion was about empowering people to affect positive transformation in their lives, and building organizational cultures that can foster personal growth.

The personal development of our staff had a direct effect on the quality of care, bottom line, the degree of satisfaction among them, and happiness among our patients. What we started noticing was that most of the innovators who took on initiatives to advance the company were those who were engaged in their own personal growth.

At that point, I was at a crossroads between growing my business or divesting it. I looked in the mirror and asked myself, *Would you like to be remembered for the kingdom you built, or for the passion that consumed your life and created your unique contribution and impact?*

It was apparent to me that my business was providing me with a platform to contribute my purpose, and to impact people and leaders positively through my organization. It came with a plethora of demands, risks, and financial rewards, which occupied a lot of my time. I decided to divest and dedicate my time to effecting change through my passion, through my writings, workshops, coaching, and engagements. What mattered to me was reaching people and leaders beyond the scope of my organization. This prompted me to write my first book, *The Dolphin's Dance*, in the field of self-discovery and conscious awareness. The reason for publishing my first book in personal transformation is my deep belief that what is in the boardroom is in the living room. We don't transplant our personality when we go to work; we are the same person with the same identity. My nagging intuition was about divesting the business instead of keeping it and delegating its operations. I followed my intuition and divested at the right time from a regulatory perspective. I feel that when I follow my intuition the stars line up to manifest my deepest desire.

Relaxation, meditation, breathing, and taking your mind off a decision you are struggling with will help you look at it differently. If you associate your wants with an emotion of pleasure, you can manifest anything you want by directing your emotion, just as we learned previously. The secret to manifest from the future is to envision what you want, then program your emotion to align with your vision as you execute smartly. This ensures your desire is for the greater good.

Great leaders similarly develop their business intuition. This helps them with their decision-making process, especially when they gamble or speculate on a certain course of action. Intuition gives them more clarity in the process, a higher chance for success, and the tools to communicate their proposal.

Should you have a gut feeling that's different from the direction your reason is pointing to regarding future actions or projects, I recommend you stop and listen to what your intuition is telling you. You may need to gather more data and perform another due diligence on the future endeavor before you proceed.

Intuition is also particularly useful in detecting dissonance within your relationships. It can inform you about the quality of the people you are recruiting or dealing with beyond their resumés.

Beyond decision-making, your intuition can guide you and direct you to emerge from the future. Learning to trust it is a leap of faith. It's like you are listening to your future self whispering to you about the direction you need to take to emerge from the future, even though some of these steps may appear unreasonable to you.

EXERCISE: USE YOUR INTUITION IN FUTURE DECISION-MAKING.

Step 1.

Sit quietly and move into a state of relaxation. State your intention of going into a deep state of relaxation, and opening yourself to connect with your intuition. Think of a project or an idea that you hesitate about. It may have been a project of yours for a long time, but you don't need to make up your mind about it.

Step 2.

Breathe in, to the count of four, hold your breath to the count of four, breathe out to the count of four, and repeat a few times. While doing this, visualize a gold light coming down from the space above your head and covering you like a veil with its warmth and brightness. Visualize each one of your organs, limbs, and extremities caressed gently by the gold light.

Step 3.

Close your eyes as you turn your eyelids upward towards the middle of your eyebrows. Try to sense how your breath is moving down to your belly and moving up to your head.

Step 4.

As you breathe, count backwards from 100 to 1 while visualizing relaxing scenes—for example, a beach, mountain scenes, a lagoon, etc. Long before you reach 1, you may drift into a deep state of relaxation.

Step 5.

Think of the project that you hesitate about.

Step 6.

Imagine yourself undertaking your project. Picture yourself, one month after, one year after, and three years after commencing the project.

Step 7.

Describe your feelings now: are you happy, at ease, relaxed, or tense and upset?

Your feeling now informs you of the answer to your dilemma. If you feel relaxed and happy, your inner self is giving you the green light and

When you access your intuition, you can unleash a force stronger than you realize. It can help you manifest from your future, even if your mind is telling you otherwise.

I hardly make any decision without checking with my gut feelings about it. This process can also help you with recruiting new staff, partners, and relationships.

One important caveat to this process is to make sure you don't fall in the trap of your unconscious bias blind spot. If the affinity to a solution confirms an old belief of yours, you are still under the influence of your past experiences. If your intuition feels like a sensation from a future occurrence, however, then you're being guided to leap into the future in a way that aligns with your passion and your purpose. Consequently, your decisions can move you and your business forward.

ORDINARY LEADERS VERSUS LEAPERS

There is nothing wrong with being an ordinary leader and leading an ordinary life, but there is great fulfillment in being an ordinary human being and leading an extraordinary life. There is great satisfaction in leaping beyond success, contributing, and impacting society. Here's how we differentiate ordinary leaders from leapers. They both have skills to lead, but the latter leap beyond themselves.

ORDINARY LEADERS	LEAPERS
Preoccupied with self wins and personal acquisitions	Preoccupied with the triple-win: I win / you win / society wins
Main motivation is personal and financial success	Personal and financial success are metrics and means to go beyond the self
The means justify the ends	The means are as important as the ends
Personal goals and missions are the key	Alignment of goals with greater purpose is the key
Future is given from the past experience	Future is generated from the future
Do not like to change their beliefs	Are willing to challenge their beliefs
Personal mission is for personal gains	Personal mission is aligned with the greater good
Do not like to share their skills or secrets of their success	They like to coach and invest in others around them to succeed
Do not like change	Adapt easily to change
Do not like to deal with emotions	Like to understand and manage emotions
Financial earnings are the ultimate measure of success	Passion and fulfillment are the ultimate measure of success
Execute in order to have more	Execute in order to impact more
Vulnerability is considered a weakness	Vulnerability is considered an authenticity
Are quick to justify their actions when things go wrong	Are quick to take on responsibilities when things go wrong
Conformity is encouraged and rewarded	Innovation is encouraged and rewarded
Short win is the motivator	Creating a legacy is the motivator

LEAPING COLLECTIVELY INTO THE FUTURE

Leaping collectively into the future is a practice of consciously accessing being, when leadership is generated from a future possibility aligned with our true self and guided by our shared collective wisdom. The leap occurs when our inner purpose meets the collective purpose and aligns with higher wisdom.

In *The Essentials of Theory U*, Otto Scharmer of MIT argues that evolution follows consciousness. As one starts shifting how one sees the system from being out there to seeing the system as self-inclusive, one starts adding another dimension to one's perception, which Scharmer calls "presencing." We start perceiving, intuiting, envisioning, and allowing knowledge to emerge from the future. This is when evolutionary thinking and institutional innovations start to align with the collective wisdom, because we start "presencing" information far beyond our own consciousness or what we thought was possible.[13]

Leaders can then start focusing on how individuals, groups, and organizations can actualize their highest future potentials and how they can become agents of creative intelligence.

Leading from the future becomes possible if this leadership is anchored in Conscious Awareness. As leaders become more consciously aware, they become the cause in creating subtle shifts of awareness in how the team starts seeing and relating to themselves, each other, to the organization, and to the collective good. This shift will create a switch from seeing the organization as one being out there, to seeing it from a perspective that includes one's own self.

Leaders start contributing more to the world by changing the rules by which they live, and by impacting global policies leading to a future that was not going to happen without them. They

---

13   Scharmer, *Essentials of Theory U*, 62.

shape the future, not as a natural progression but as a leap in the cycle, and actively participate in a better one for all. It is going beyond their ability to manage people, but to consciously co-create with them a present reality from a vision of a fully realized future.

Leap from the Future

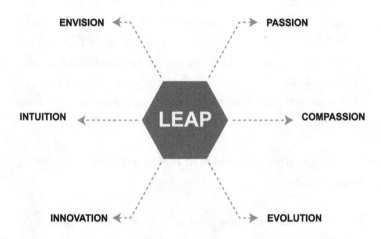

For the triple-win paradigm of leadership to materialize, it must transform beyond the follower to the society we live in, shifting our mindset and emotion-set from one of immediate gratification to a more sustainable and consciously aware per-spective and approach.

Right now, we are all witnessing the crumbling of the old para-digm and the emergence of a new one. Individuals have started redefining themselves and their vision. Followers started to shift their aspiration from emulating their leaders' behavior, achieve-ments, success, power, fame, and influence to lead from a deeper place of beingness. They started aspiring to lead with a higher purpose and humanity. The uprise of powerful and successful women and men leaders is happening, and women are called to rise more, embrace their roles, and redefine their leadership style.

When we envision, intuit, and innovate with compassion, we evolve. When we shift to include social impact, we will thrive.

As capitalism shifts to include social responsibility and sustainability, humanity will begin to thrive. When trust bankers include social impact as part of their investments, they will no longer finance businesses that compromise the collective well. Individuals at their own levels become more aware of where their financial managers are investing, and veto investment in weapons of mass destruction or environmental harms.

What style of women and men leaders will shape our future, from the future?

Those who lead from their passion, and who have a vision for a new world that guarantees a triple-win paradigm. Leaders who are emotionally intelligent, compassionate, vulnerable, intuitive, and empathic. Those who exhibit such characteristics and execute their vision and mission, while aligning their actions to match them. Those who can express their purpose and contribute it to the greater good. It is not about the competitive edge of top performers or the skillsets of successful leaders. It is about developing the qualities and abilities that allow them to become aligned with the field of their own creation—Leaning into their Passion, Executing their Purpose, Aligning their Mindset, Processing their Emotions, and becoming leapers. Since these qualities are rooted in love and compassion, the net positive impact on society is sustainability, harmony, and success—a win-win-win. They can create viable organizations, systems, and teams engaged in missions beyond their self-interest while being successful and fulfilled. These leaders can generate a movement towards a positive social and global evolution. They collectively leap from the future!

KEY TAKEAWAYS

- Applying the four L.E.A.P steps in your everyday life will enable you to leap without fear of criticism or failure, with total confidence in your vision and your abilities, and in total harmony with the external systems around you.
- Evolve, innovate, and leap from the future. A leap could bypass the normal progression, and create an evolutionary great jump from one level to an unimagined one.
- Leap into the triple-win paradigm: you win / I win / the world wins.
- Compassion is a key to transform fear and make space to leap.
- The love and compassion we seek must begin within.
- The secret to manifest from the future is to envision what you want, then program your emotion to align with your vision as you execute smartly while ensuring your desire is for the greater good.
- Use unbiased intuition to sense, discern, and empower the decision-making from the future.
- Ordinary Leaders versus Leapers. Leaping into the future: when we envision, intuit, and innovate with compassion, we evolve. When we shift to include social impact, we thrive.
- We start to leap collectively when our evolutionary thinking and institutional innovations align with the collective wisdom.

A FINAL NOTE

A LEADERSHIP WAITING TO BE BORN!

We are at the cusp of creating a new world. We are at a cross-roads between creating a positive world that works for all or a negative destructive one. We are all responsible for this creation and none of us is off the hook by virtue of living in it.

So, let's envision it, and start to practice it through the four L.E.A.P. steps. Then, let's collectively leap to it!

Imagine a world driven by our emerging future instead of being driven by the past!

Imagine a world inspired by our highest potential instead of a current reality driven by our limitations!

Imagine a world where leadership is expressed from a limitless depth of being instead of a leadership expressed from a sense of lack and "never enough-ness!"

Imagine a leadership manifested from the true self and higher calling instead of a leadership manifested from the ego-made self, constantly threatened and restless!

Imagine a world co-created from our intuited future instead of a default world generated from our past programs!

A world moved by the power of compassion instead of the power of greed!

A world enthused from our connectivity and not from the worship of our individual self!

A world where leadership is not about the one person at the top but is inclusive to all!

A world led by leaders who are committed to peace and collaboration instead of leaders of power and ego!

This world is right now utopic, yet this world exists as a possibility in the consciousness that we programmed to access together during this work.

Some may still think that we are imagining a utopian world. Remember the time when we sent letters and waited for answers in the mail? If someone told us that we would communicate in a split second via the Internet, we would have been shocked! It was only in the 1990s that the Internet explosion began. Do you see yourself operating in the world without it today? It was unthinkable back then to be connected to all the people you know via social media. It was impossible to purchase all your goods with a click. We probably would have thought that it was pure fiction.

As we stand on the edge of big realizations, our old institutions and values are crumbling; our old beliefs don't serve us anymore. Some of our past foundation is dilapidated, and we are ready for a new start. Why not believe that our starting point could be a leadership based in conscious awareness and a process beginning with us?

If we leap one at a time, we will create the great leap all together. Leaders lead to create success; leapers leap to create a better future for all.

Waking up to our own leadership is the first step towards evolving leadership in the world. If we look at the world's picture, the challenges and disagreements are intense. We can feel overwhelmed, discouraged, and helpless. But if we rise to the occasion of transforming the way we lead our life and engage in the four steps of this book, we will be marching towards a better world together. We will be transcending egotistic, ethnic, political, religious, economic, and previous programming to create and design a new destiny for us that will impact the ecosystem in general.

Unleashing the leader within us and letting it shine is our own call to action. Once untethered, there is no turning back. It is like telling Michelangelo to stop sculpting his *David* when he was in the middle of it. What started as his creation at age twenty-six became the perfect symbol of Florence, and ours to enjoy, admire, and be inspired by for generations to come. Artistically, Michelangelo delivered his sculpture from his passion, and created the balance, harmony, and realistic form that he was acclaimed for. Whether the church saw the Biblical figure in it, the politicians a symbol of strength and defiance, or the artists a symbol of what was possible, each found a personal symbol that had nothing to do with the creation.

Like Michelangelo, we can all sculpt our own David and contribute to it at our level. It really does not matter what scale you are operating at: leading your life, raising your family, running a big enterprise or company, or leading a nation. What matters is your net impact on the world, and knowing that you can affect it positively by adding value to it.

Apply the tools that you have acquired in this book to execute your purpose as you declutter all hindrances in your mindset. Align it to your vision. Transform your stumbling blocks into catalysts. This is a power in your hands right now. Becoming aware of your emotional logo, practicing deprogramming your triggers, and using your emotions to manifest your vision are valuable instruments in your toolbox. Leaping beyond what you could imagine possible is your choice to make. Creating these tools was, for me, like sculpting my own David. It is my gift for you to use, generate from, build upon, and pass on. Should you decide to do so, I wish you the best journey of fulfillment, joy, success, and impact.

Whether you progress, evolve, or leap, waking up together and marching towards a new world that we sculpt together is our collective "David."

Let's wake up, let's evolve, and let's build a better future for us and those around us. Let's leap together, and let's do it now!

CPSIA information can be obtained
at www.ICGtesting.com
Printed in the USA
JSHW020523030623
42617JS00001B/7